D0456288

Pocket
REYKJAVÍK
TOP EXPERIENCES · LOCAL LIFE · MADE EASY

Alexis Averbuck

In This Book

QuickStart Guide

Your keys to understanding the city and its surrounds – we help you decide what to do and how to do it

Need to Know
Tips for a smooth trip

Neighbourhoods & Regions
What's where

Explore Reykjavík

The best things to see and do, by neighbourhood and by region

Top Experiences
Make the most of your visit

Local Life
The insider's city

The Best of Reykjavík

Highlights of the city and its surrounds in handy lists to help you plan

Best Walks
See the city on foot

Reykjavík's Best...
The best experiences

Survival Guide

Tips and tricks for a seamless, hassle-free city experience

Getting Around
Travel like a local

Essential Information
Including where to stay

Our selection of the city and region's best places to eat, drink and experience:

◎ **Experiences**

✖ **Eating**

🍷 **Drinking**

✪ **Entertainment**

🔒 **Shopping**

These symbols give you the vital information for each listing:

- ☏ Telephone Numbers
- ⊙ Opening Hours
- P Parking
- Ⓝ Nonsmoking
- @ Internet Access
- 🛜 Wi-Fi Access
- 🌱 Vegetarian Selection
- 📖 English-Language Menu
- ♿ Family-Friendly
- 🐾 Pet-Friendly
- 🚌 Bus
- ⛴ Ferry
- Ⓜ Metro
- Ⓢ Subway
- 🚋 Tram
- 🚆 Train

Find each listing quickly on maps for each neighbourhood and region:

Bar Hemingway

16 🍷 Map p233, B2

Legend has it that Hemi self, wielding a machine rate this timber-pan ered bar during showpiece is a en by Papa ar town. Dress s.com; Hôtel Rit ⊙6.30pm-2a

Lonely Planet's Reykjavík

Lonely Planet Pocket Guides are designed to get you straight to the heart of the city.

Inside you'll find all the must-see sights, plus tips to make your visit to each one really memorable. We've split the city into easy-to-navigate neighbourhoods and regions, and provided clear maps so you'll find your way around with ease. Our expert authors have searched out the best of the city: walks, food, nightlife and shopping, to name a few. Because you want to explore, our 'Local Life' pages will take you to some of the most exciting areas to experience the real Reykjavík.

And of course you'll find all the practical tips you need for a smooth trip: itineraries for short visits, how to get around, and how much to tip the guy who serves you a drink at the end of a long day's exploration.

It's your guarantee of a really great experience.

Our Promise

You can trust our travel information because Lonely Planet authors visit the places we write about, each and every edition. We never accept freebies for positive coverage, so you can rely on us to tell it like it is.

Explore Reykjavík   21

Worth a Trip:

QuickStart Guide

Welcome to Reykjavík

The world's most northerly capital combines colourful build-ings, wild nightlife and a capricious soul to brilliant effect. Imaginative Reykjavikers embrace their sense of community and bring a joy to life, creating captivating museums, cool music, and offbeat cafes and bars. Reykjavík is a superb base for touring Iceland's natural wonders: glacier-topped volcanoes, shimmering falls and black-sand beaches.

Yacht marina and Harpa concert hall (p55)
RICHARD CUMMINGS / GETTY IMAGES ©

Reykjavík & Around
Top Experiences

National Museum (p24)

Iceland's National Museum gathers together the country's most priceless arte-facts, creating a trail of clues to life at Settlement and beyond. Peruse the finds and gain insight into the hardy hearts of Icelanders.

LONELY PLANET / GETTY IMAGES ©

ARCTIC IMAGES / ALAMY ©

The Settlement Exhibition (p26)

The modern era meets the Viking longhouse at this exhibition centred around Reykjavík's oldest ruins, and souped up with fun, fascinating space-age displays.

Hallgrímskirkja (p50)

The capital's iconic church perches atop the city centre and is visible for miles around. From the heights of its modernist steeple survey the broad sweep of the city, ocean and snow-capped mountains.

Gullfoss (p82)

Thundering layers of icy water cascade over tiered rockfaces and down a narrow gorge at Iceland's iconic Gullfoss. Meaning 'Golden Falls', they live up to their name when they sparkle in sunset light.

Þingvellir (p78)

The continental plates part at historic Þingvellir, the site of the original (outdoor!) Icelandic parliament. Waterfalls gush off the rift and ancient stones mark the earliest eras of Iceland's history.

Blue Lagoon (p72)

Wash away your cares at the ethereal Blue Lagoon, the flashiest version of Icelandic hot-potting. Set in otherworldly lava fields, with its vibrant geothermal turquoise waters, there's really nothing else like it.

Geysir (p80)

Impressive Geysir rises from a bubbling geothermal field surrounded by a contrasting lush valley. Like clockwork, one of the geysers makes a swooshing whoop as it shoots boiling water into the air.

Snæfellsjökull National Park (p110)

With its beaches, lava fields and glacier crown, Snæfellsjökull National Park is one of Iceland's best escapes – as a day trip from Reykjavík or as a relaxing long weekend.

Settlement Centre (p108)

Lively Borgarnes was the site of some dramatic saga action. Its Settlement Centre brilliantly recounts the country's discovery and settlement, as well as one of its most intriguing heroes, from *Egil's Saga*.

Jökulsárlón (p104)

A sparkling procession of icebergs sheer off of Breiðamerkurjökull glacier and drift serenely through the 25-sq-km Jökulsárlón lagoon in ever-changing light, before floating by bobbing seals and out to sea.

Reykjavík & Around
Local Life

Insider tips to help you find the real city

Reykjavík is small, approachable and charming, and in an absolutely gorgeous seaside setting, but its real magic is its people. A lively, creative, unselfconscious group, they live with inspiration and insight, they play hard, and they do it all with an easy aplomb.

Djammið Nightlife
(p52)

▶ Lively bars
▶ Partying with locals

Some visitors come to Reykjavík just for its nightlife. You may not realise it, but this tiny town can get out and party. The local name for it is *djammið* – a booze-drenched parade through the central Reykjavík streets, skipping from bar to bar.

Laugardalur
(p68)

▶ Geothermal pools
▶ Parks & gardens

One of the favourite pastimes of Icelanders is a good soak and a chat at the geothermal springs.

One of the largest pools, in Laugardalur, a valley of hot springs, sits alongside a popular spa, botanic gardens, a bustling children's park and excellent local art museums.

Viðey Island
(p70)

▶ Secluded island
▶ Coastal views

Little Viðey Island, just offshore from Reykjavík, was one of the first spots settled in Iceland. Now an uninhabited, dreamy haven, it's dotted with unique art installations and criss-crossed by lovely walking and cycling tracks – a favourite quick getaway for Reykjavikers.

Reykjanes Peninsula
(p74)

▶ Windswept villages
▶ Volcanic landscapes

Yes, the Reykjanes Peninsula is home to the famous Blue Lagoon, but locals know it's also a land of fishing villages and lonely lighthouses, dramatic cliffs and migrating seabirds. You'll find Reykjavikers hiking or ATV-ing along its mineral lakes, volcanoes, beaches and rugged lava fields.

Laugardalur (p68)

Reykjavík nightclub

Other great places to experience the city like a local:

Reykjavík
Day Planner

Day One

☀ Explore the Old Reykjavík quarter, taking in the **Ráðhús** (city hall; p30) and **Alþingi** (parliament; p30) at lake **Tjörnin** (p29), then peruse the city's best museums, such as the **National Museum** (p24), **Reykjavík Art Museum** (p29) or **The Settlement Exhibition** (p26), built around a Viking longhouse. Lunch at hip **Nora Magasin** (p34), or grab a beer at **Café Paris** (p27).

☀ Wander up arty Skólavörðustígur, shop for the latest Icelandic music at **12 Tónar** (p64), then photograph immense church **Hallgrímskirkja** (p50). Stroll Laugavegur, with shops such as **Kiosk** (p65) and **Kraum** (p64), or bookshop **Mál og Menning** (p66). Alternatively, take a dip at **Sundhöllin** (p57) then examine the extraordinary **Icelandic Phallological Museum** (p56).

☾ Enjoy people-watching and drinks at **Bravó** (p62) or **Kaldi** (p52). Restaurants such as **Vegamót** (p60), **Public House** (p60) and **KEX** (p62) turn into night-time party hang-outs, perfect for joining Reykjavík's pub-crawl **djammið** (p52). Don't miss favourite **Kaffibarinn** (p53) or beer-lovers' **Skúli Craft Bar** (p35). Wrap up with a late-night dance session at **Kiki** (p53), **Prikið** (p53) or **Paloma** (p35).

Day Two

☀ After a late night out, brunch at **Bergsson Mathús** (p33), **Grái Kötturinn** (p59) or **Laundromat Café** (p34). Then head over to the **Old Harbour** (p38) for its museums, such as the **Víkin Maritime Museum** (p41) or **Saga Museum** (p41), and a whale-watching tour. If sailing the open seas gets you hungry for lunch, grab a grilled fish skewer at **Sægreifinn** (p44).

☀ Visit **Laugardalur** (p68), east of the centre, for a soak at the geothermal pools, gardens, idyllic **Café Flóra** (p69) and cool art. Or rent a bike and ferry out to historic **Viðey Island** (p70), where you can cruise between art installations and fishing-village ruins.

☾ Book ahead for a swanky evening at a top Icelandic restaurant, such as **Dill** (p58), **Messinn** (p32) or **Matur og Drykkur** (p43), then hit a cocktail bar such as **Apotek** (p32), **Slippbarinn** (p47) or **Loftið** (p35). Alternatively, try Reykjavík's most revered hot dogs at **Bæjarins Beztu** (p32), then catch a show at **Harpa** (p55) or **Mengi** (p64), an Icelandic movie at **Bíó Paradís** (p64) or live music at **Café Rosenberg** (p64) or **Húrra** (p36).

Short on time?
We've arranged Reykjavík's must-sees into these day-by-day itineraries to make sure you see the very best of the city in the time you have available.

Day Three

If you've got the time and can rent your own wheels, you can extend these country stops. Day tours are also a popular, effective option. Get an early start with the famous **Golden Circle** (p76). Explore the rift and historic parliament site at **Þingvellir** (p78) then lunch in Laugarvatn on delicious local fare at **Lindin** (p88).

Stroll around the spouting **Geysir** (p80) and the thundering cascade **Gullfoss** (p82). If possible, leave time for **river rafting** (p88) out of Reykholt or a soak at the natural, restored spring at **Gamla Laugin** (p85) in Flúðir.

If you're tired, head home, stopping for dinner at **Tryggvaskáli** (p89) in Selfoss or **Varma** (p89) in Hveragerði. If not, use your car to go to the shore for seafood at sleepy fishing villages **Stokkseyri** and **Eyrarbakki** (p96). Or, if you haven't the time to visit the **Blue Lagoon** (p73) coming or going from the airport, go late this evening, after the crowds have dwindled, before returning to Reykjavík.

Day Four

Choose between the wonderful West or the famous South. If you're going to West Iceland, spend the morning at Borgarnes' **Settlement Centre** (p108) learning about Icelandic history and *Egil's Saga*. If you're heading South, drive to Hella or Hvolsvöllur for **horse riding** (p97), or all the way to Skógar via its marvellous falls **Seljalandsfoss** and **Gljúfurárbui** (p96). Catch an amphibious bus or join a super-Jeep trip to **Þórsmörk** (p100), or take a guided walk on **Sólheimajökull** (p97).

In the West, choose between exploring inland lava tubes at **Viðgelmir** (p115) and the interior of a glacier at **Langjökull** (p113), or hiking, whale watching and glacier walking in **Snæfellsjökull National Park** (p110). In the South, shoot out to Vík for black basalt beach **Reynisfjara** (p96) and enormous rock arch landmark **Dyrhólaey** (p96).

In the West, finish with dinner in Grundarfjörður at **Bjargarsteinn Mathús** (p118) or Stykkishólmur at **Plássið** (p120) or **Narfeyrarstofa** (p119). In the South, barrel up the northeast coast, through otherworldly lanscapes, to the incredible glacier tongues descending from **Vatnajökull**, and fantastical glacier lagoon **Jökulsárlón**.

Need to Know

**For more information,
see Survival Guide (p143)**

Currency
Icelandic króna (kr)

Language
Icelandic; English widely spoken

Visas
Generally not required for stays of up
to 90 days. Member of the Schengen
Convention.

Money
Credit cards reign supreme, even in the
most rural reaches of the country (PIN
required for some purchases, such as
petrol). ATMs available in all towns.

Mobile Phones
Mobile coverage widespread. Visitors
with GSM phones can make roaming
calls; purchase a local SIM card if you're
staying a while.

Time
Western European Time Zone (GMT/UTC,
same as London), but there's no daylight
saving time.

Tipping
As service and VAT are always included in
prices, tipping isn't required in Iceland.

① Before You Go

Your Daily Budget

Budget: Less than kr25,000
▶ Dorm bed: kr5000–7000
▶ Grill-bar grub/soup lunch: kr1600–2200
▶ Golden Circle bus pass: kr10,600

Midrange: kr25,000–40,000
▶ Guesthouse double room: kr19,000–25,000
▶ Cafe meal: kr1800–4000
▶ Small vehicle rental per day: kr10,000

Top End: More than kr40,000
▶ Boutique double room: kr30,000–50,000
▶ Main dish in top restaurant: kr4000–7000
▶ 4WD rental per day: kr25,000

Useful Websites

Visit Iceland (www.visiticeland.com)
Official tourism portal.

Visit Reykjavík (www.visitreykjavik.is) Official
site for the capital.

Reykjavík Grapevine (www.grapevine.is)
Great English-language newspaper/website.

Iceland Review (www.icelandreview.com)
News, current affairs, entertainment and more.

Lonely Planet (www.lonelyplanet.com/
iceland) Destination information, hotel bookings, traveller forum and more.

Advance Planning

Three to six months before Book all
accommodation in Reykjavík and beyond.
Demand always outstrips supply.

One month before Book adventure or bus
tours in the countryside.

One week before Reserve tables at top
restaurants. Prebook the airport bus, and
Blue Lagoon (p72) tickets if you want to hit
the lagoon on arrival.

② Arriving in Reykjavík

Iceland's primary international airport, Keflavík International airport (KEF) is 48km west of Reykjavík, on the Reykjanes Peninsula. Frequent, convenient buses serve central Reykjavík.

✈ From Keflavík International Airport

Bus Flybus (☎580 5400; www.re.is; 📶), Airport Express (☎540 1313; www.airportexpress.is; 📶) and Airport Direct (☎497 5000; www.reykjaviksightseeing.is/airport-direct; 📶) have buses and minibuses connecting the airport with Reykjavík (50 minutes). They all offer pick-up/drop-off at many accommodations; kids get discounted fares. Flybus also serves the Blue Lagoon. Strætó (www.bus.is) bus 55 also connects the BSÍ bus terminal and the airport (kr1680, nine daily Monday to Friday in summer).

Taxis Cost around kr15,000.

✈ At the Airport

Iceland's primary international airport, **Keflavík International Airport** (KEF: ☎525 6000; www.kefairport.is) has ATMs, money exchange, car hire, an **information desk** (☎425 0330, booking service ☎570 7799; www.visitreykjanes.is; ⏰6am-8pm Mon-Fri, noon-5pm Sat & Sun) and cafes. The duty-free shops in the arrival area sell liquor at far better prices than you'll find in town. There's also a desk for collecting duty-free cash back from eligible purchases in Iceland. The 10-11 convenience store sells SIM cards, and major tour companies such as Reykjavík Excursions and Grey Line have desks.

③ Getting Around

A car is unnecessary in central Reykjavík as it's so easy to explore on foot and by bus. Car and camper hire are best for countryside excursions.

🚌 Local Buses

Strætó (www.bus.is) operates regular, easy buses around Reykjavík and its suburbs; it also operates long-distance buses. It has online schedules and a smartphone app. Many free maps like *Welcome to Reykjavík City Map* also include bus-route maps.

The fare is kr420 and can be paid on board (no change given). Buses run from 7am until 11pm or midnight daily (from 11am on Sunday). A limited night-bus service runs until 2am on Friday and Saturday.

🚗 Car

The most common way for visitors to get around outside of Reykjavík. They're pricey to hire but provide great freedom. A 2WD vehicle will get you almost everywhere in summer (note: not into the highlands, or on F roads). Summer-only 4WD buses go to the highlands, otherwise you'll need a 4WD or a tour. Cars are available at both the international and domestic airports, the BSÍ bus terminal and some city locations.

🚌 Regional Buses

Iceland has a decent bus network operating from around mid-May to mid-September between major destinations. Outside these months services are less frequent (or nonexistent). The free *Public Transport in Iceland* map (www.publictransport.is) has a good overview of routes.

✈ Regional Flights

If you're short on time, domestic flights from the central **Reykjavík Domestic Airport** (Reykjavíkurflugvöllur; www.reykjavikairport.is; Innanlandsflug) help maximise your stay.

Reykjavík
Neighbourhoods

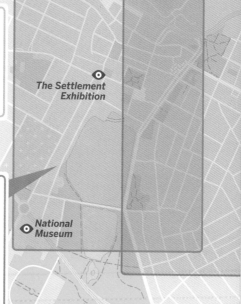

Old Harbour (p38)
Once primarily a working harbour, this pretty, lively district now offers a fun cluster of museums and eateries, and is the launch-point for whale-watching boats.

The Settlement Exhibition

Old Reykjavík (p22)
Reykjavík's ancient heart lies here, with its remains of a Viking longhouse, interesting architecture and top museums.

◉ Top Experiences
National Museum
The Settlement Exhibition

National Museum

Laugavegur & Skólavörðustígur (p48)

Laugavegur is Reykjavík's premier shopping street and centre for cool cafes, bars and restaurants. Its arty cousin Skóla-vörðustígur leads to famous Hallgrímskirkja.

⊙ Top Experiences

Hallgrímskirkja

Golden Circle (p76)

⊙ Top Experiences

Þingvellir

Geysir

Gullfoss

West Iceland (p106)

⊙ Top Experiences

Settlement Centre

Snæfellsjökull National Park

South Coast (p92)

Worth a Trip

⊙ Top Experiences

Blue Lagoon

Jökulsárlón

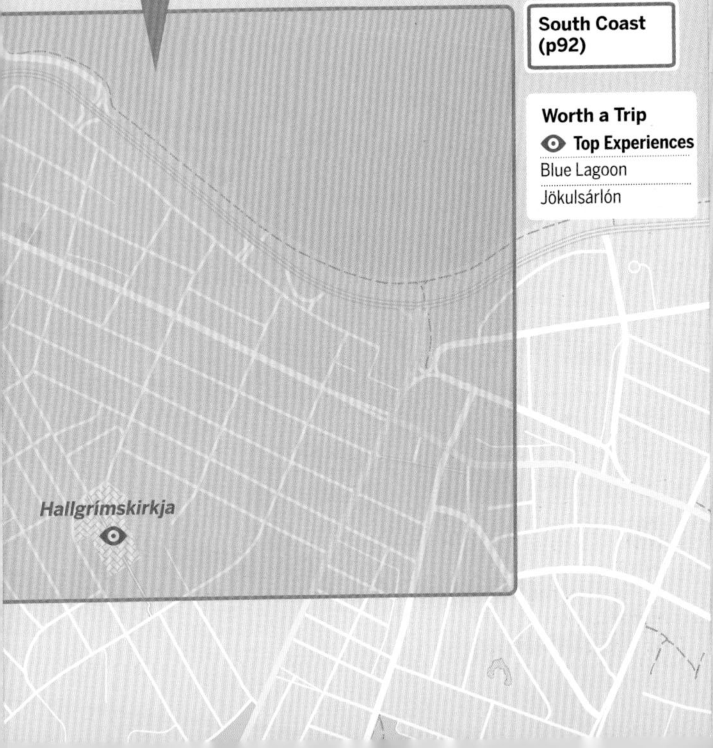

Hallgrímskirkja
⊙

Explore
Reykjavík

Worth a Trip

View over Reykjavík from Hallgrímskirkja (p50)
TSUGULIEV / SHUTTERSTOCK ©

Explore

Old Reykjavík

The area dubbed Old Reykjavík is the jaunty heart of the capital. Anchored by placid Tjörnin, the city-centre lake, the neighbourhood is loaded with brightly coloured residential houses and a series of great sights and interesting historic buildings. Old Reykjavík is also tops for a wander: from the seafront to Austurvöllur park, Alþingi (parliament) and Ráðhús (city hall) and on to the National Museum.

MARTIN M303 / SHUTTERSTOCK ©

The Sights in a Day

☀ Get an early start at the **Reykjavík Art Museum – Hafnarhús** (p29) or the **Reykjavík Museum of Photography** (p30) for the city's best contemporary art, then stroll up through the oldest parts of town around **Austurvöllur** (p30), where you'll find the **Alþingi** (p30) and **Raðhús** (p30) on the edge of pretty **Tjörnin** (p29) lake. Visit the Viking longhouse and high-tech exhibits at **The Settlement Exhibition** (p26) before heading to lunch at **Bergsson Mathús** (p33) or **Nora Magasin** (p34).

☀ Walk through the lake's parks or hop a bus to reach the absorbing **National Museum** (p24). Spend the afternoon perusing the country's most precious artefacts, while learning about its history.

☾ Head back to the centre for a fantastic dinner at **Messinn** (p32), **Apotek** (p32) or **Grill-markaðurinn** (p32) or a casual meal at **Icelandic Fish & Chips** (p34) or **Laundromat Café** (p34), then tip back brews at **Micro Bar** (p34), or dress up for fine cocktails at **Loftið** (p35). Catch live bands at **Húrra** (p36), before late-night dancing at **Paloma** (p35) or nightcap hot dogs at **Bæjarins Beztu** (p32).

⦿ Top Experiences

National Museum (p24)

The Settlement Exhibition (p26)

♥ Best of Reykjavík

Eating
Messinn (p32)

Apotek (p32)

Grillmarkaðurinn (p32)

Bæjarins Beztu (p32)

Lobster Hut (p34)

Museums, Exhibitions & Galleries
Reykjavík Art Museum – Hafnarhús (p29)

Reykjavík Museum of Photography (p30)

Volcano House (p30)

i8 (p30)

Getting There

➊ **On Foot** Central Reykjavík is super-compact and walkable. You'll get to most places on foot.

🚌 **Bus** City buses 1, 3, 6, 11, 12, 13 and 14 from Hlemmur all stop in Old Reykjavík at Lækjartorg and Ráðhús.

🚌 **Bus** Bus 14 connects Laugardalur, Hlemmur and Old Reykjavík, and the Old Harbour.

Top Experiences
National Museum

The superb National Museum beautifully displays Icelandic artefacts from settlement to the modern age, providing a meaningful overview of Iceland's history and culture. Brilliantly curated exhibits lead you through the struggle to settle and organise the forbidding island, the radical changes wrought by the advent of Christianity, the lean times of domination by foreign powers to Iceland's eventual independence.

👁 Map p28, A5

📞 530 2200

www.nationalmuseum.is

Suðurgata 41

adult/child kr1500/free

🕙 10am-5pm May–mid-Sep, closed Mon mid-Sep–Apr

🚌 1, 3, 6, 12, 14

Settlement Era Finds

The premier section of the museum describes the Settlement Era, and features swords, meticulously carved **drinking horns** (pictured below left), and **silver hoards**. A powerful **bronze figure of Thor** is thought to date to about 1000.

Domestic Life

Exhibits explain how the chieftains ruled and how people survived on little, lighting their dark homes and fashioning bog iron. There's everything from the remains of early *skyr* (yoghurt-like dessert) production to intricate pendants and brooches. Look for the Viking-era **hnefatafl game set** (a bit like chess); this artefact's discovery in a grave in Baldursheimar led to the founding of the museum.

Viking Graves

Encased in the floor, you'll find Viking-era graves, with their precious burial goods: horse bones, a sword, pins, a ladle, a comb. One of the tombs, containing an eight-month-old infant, is the only one of its kind ever found.

Ecclesiastical Artefacts

The section of the museum that details the introduction of Christianity is chock-a-block with rare art and artefacts, for example, the priceless 13th-century **Valþjófsstaðir church door**.

The Modern Era

Upstairs, collections span from 1600 to today and give a clear sense of how Iceland struggled under foreign rule, finally gained independence and went on to modernise. Look for the **papers and belongings of Jón Sigurðsson**, the architect of Iceland's independence.

JOE VOGAN / ALAMY ©

☑ Top Tips

▶ The excellent audioguide (kr300) adds loads of useful detail. The one for kids is in Icelandic or English only.

▶ Leave a little extra time for the museum's rotating photographic exhibitions.

▶ Free English tours run at 11am on Wednesdays, Saturdays and Sundays from May to mid-September.

▶ It's a bit out of the way; hop on bus 1, 3, 6, 12 or 14 to reach the museum.

✕ Take a Break

The museum's ground-floor cafe offers wi-fi and a welcome respite, with wraparound windows looking out on a flowing fountain. It serves a full range of coffee drinks, and wholesome soups, sandwiches and salads (snacks kr600 to 1800).

Otherwise you'll need to hop a bus back into the centre for food.

Top Experiences
The Settlement Exhibition

This fascinating archaeological ruin-museum is based around a 10th-century Viking longhouse and other Settlement Era finds from central Reykjavík. Fine exhibitions imaginatively combine technological wizardry and archaeology to give a glimpse into early Icelandic life. Excavations in the area are ongoing and on-site curators and archaeo-anthropologists have a passion for bringing history to life.

👁 Map p28, B2

Landnámssýningin

📞 411 6370

www.reykjavikmuseum.is

Aðalstræti 16

adult/child kr1500/free

🕐 9am-6pm

Boundary wall of the longhouse

Viking Longhouse

The entire museum is constructed around a 10th-century Viking longhouse unearthed here on Aðalstræti from 2001 to 2002. Mainly a series of foundation walls now, it was thought to be inhabited for only 60 years. Exhibits to look out for are areas with animal bones deliberately built into the structure (for good fortune, perhaps), and the old spring.

Boundary Wall

Tephra layers are the layer of fragments from a volcanic eruption, and are used to date sites around Iceland. The longhouse was built on top of the 871 layer, but don't miss the fragment of boundary wall at the back of the museum, which was found *below* the tephra layer, and is thus older still. It's the oldest human-made structure in Reykjavík.

Ancient Artefacts

Arcing around the side of the exhibit, softly lit niches contain artefacts found in the area, ranging from great auk bones (a bird now extinct) to fish-oil lamps and an iron axe. The latest finds from ancient workshops near the current Alþingi include a silver bracelet and a spindle whorl (for making thread) inscribed with runes (reading 'Vilborg owns me').

High-Tech Displays

Among the captivating high-tech displays are interactive multimedia tables explaining the area's excavations, which span several city blocks; a wraparound panorama showing how things would have looked at the time of the longhouse; and a space-age-feeling panel that allows you to steer through different layers of the longhouse's construction.

☑ **Top Tips**

▶ Excellent English-language tours run at 11am on weekdays from June to August.

▶ Multilingual audio-guides are free.

▶ The museum's fun kids' corner has traditional Icelandic toys, rune spelling exercises and computer games.

✕ **Take a Break**

Stroll up to the area just north of Tjörnin to wholesome Bergsson Mathús (p33) for a casual lunch or brunch, popular with locals.

Head to the Austurvöllur Sq area, where cafes and bars such as **Café Paris** (Map p28, C2; ☑ 551 1020; www.cafeparis.is; Austurstræti 14; mains kr2800-6000; ☺8am-midnight Sun-Thu, to 1am Fri & Sat; ☎) spill onto the park in warmer months.

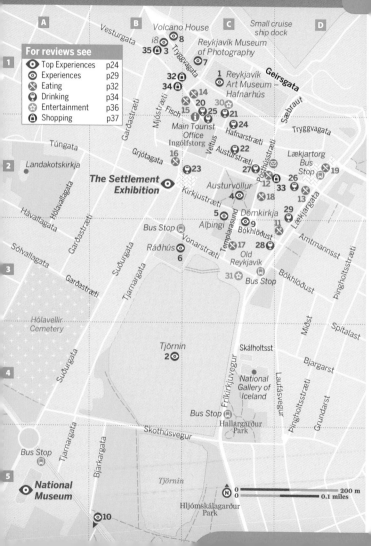

A

B

Vesturgata

Volcano House

C

Small cruise ship dock

D

i8 🔘 8
35 🔒 3

Tryggvagata

Reykjavík Museum of Photography

7

Geirsgata

32 🔒

34 🔒

15 🔘 14

20

30 ✪

1 Reykjavík Art Museum – Hafnarhús

Sæbraut

1

Garðastræti

Miðstræti

Fisch

25 🔘 21

24

22

Main Tourist Office
Ingólfstorg

Hafnarstræti

Tryggvagata

Lækjartorg Bus Stop

19

Túngata

Garðastræti

Grjótagata

16

23

Austurstræti

Veltus

27

12

33

26

Lækjargata

Landakotskirkja

The Settlement Exhibition 🔘

Kirkjustræti

Austurvöllur

4

18

13

Hávallagata

Hólavallagata

Dómkirkja

29

Sólvallagata

Garðastræti

Bus Stop

5

Alþingi

Vonarstræti

Templarasund

9

Bókhlöðust

11

Lækjargata

Amtmannsst

Garðastræti

Suðurgata

Tjarnargata

Ráðhús

6

17

31

28

Old Reykjavík

Bus Stop

Bókhlöðust

Þingholtsstræti

3

Hólavellir Cemetery

Tjörnin

2

Skálholtsst

Miðst

Spítalast

Fríkirkjuvegur

National Gallery of Iceland

Bjargarst

4

Suðurgata

Laufásvegur

Þingholtsstræti

Grundarst

Bus Stop

Skothúsvegur

Hallargarður Park

Bus Stop

5

National Museum 🔘

Tjarnargata

Bjarkargata

Tjörnin

0 ————— 200 m
N ⊙
0 ————— 0.1 miles

10 🔘

Hljómskálagarður Park

GODDARD PHOTOGRAPHY / GETTY IMAGES ©

Reykjavík Art Museum – Hafnarhús

Experiences

Reykjavík Art Museum – Hafnarhús

ART MUSEUM

1 ◉ Map p28, C1

Reykjavík Art Museum's Hafnarhús is a marvellously restored warehouse converted into a soaring steel-and-concrete exhibition space. Though the well-curated exhibitions of cutting-edge contemporary Icelandic art change frequently (think installations, videos, paintings and sculpture), you can always count on an area with the comic-book-style paintings of Erró (Guðmundur Guðmundsson), a political artist who has donated several thousand works to the museum.

The **cafe**, run by Frú Lauga farmers market (p69), has great harbour views. (☎ 411 6400; www.artmuseum.is; Tryggvagata 17; adult/child kr1500/free; ⊙10am-5pm Fri-Wed, to 10pm Thu)

Tjörnin

LAKE

2 ◉ Map p28, B4

This placid lake at the centre of the city is sometimes locally called the Pond. It echoes with the honks and squawks of over 40 species of visiting birds, including swans, geese and Arctic terns; feeding the ducks is a popular pastime for the under-fives. Pretty sculpture-dotted parks including **Hljómskála-garður** (admission free) line the southern shores, and their paths are much used by cyclists and joggers. In winter, hardy souls strap on ice skates and turn the lake into an **outdoor rink**.

i8
GALLERY

 3 Map p28, B1

This gallery represents some of the country's top modern artists, many of whom show overseas as well. (551 3666; www.i8.is; Tryggvagata 16; admission free; ☺11am-5pm Tue-Fri, 1-5pm Sat)

Austurvöllur
PARK

 4 Map p28, C2

Grassy Austurvöllur was once part of first-settler Ingólfur Arnarson's hay fields. Today it's a favourite spot for cafe lounging or lunchtime picnics and summer sunbathing next to the Alþingi, and is sometimes used for open-air concerts and political demonstrations. The statue in the centre is of Jón Sigurðsson, who led the campaign for Icelandic independence.

Alþingi
HISTORIC BUILDING

5 Map p28, C2

Iceland's first parliament, the Alþingi, was created at Þingvellir in AD 930. After losing its independence in the 13th century, the country gradually won back its autonomy, and the modern Alþingi building moved into this current basalt building in 1881; a stylish glass-and-stone annexe was completed in 2002. Visitors can attend **sessions** (four times weekly mid-September to early June; see website for details)

when parliament is sitting. (Parliament; 563 0500; www.althingi.is; Kirkjustraeti; admission free)

Ráðhús
NOTABLE BUILDING

6 Map p28, B3

Reykjavík's waterside Ráðhús is a beautifully positioned postmodern construction of concrete stilts, tinted windows and mossy walls rising from Tjörnin. Inside there's an interesting 3D topographical map of Iceland. (Vonarstræti; admission free; ☺8am-4pm Mon-Fri)

Reykjavík Museum of Photography
MUSEUM

7 Map p28, C1

This gallery room above Reykjavík City Library is worth a visit for its top-notch exhibitions of regional photographers. If you take the lift up, descend by the stairs, which are lined with vintage black-and-white photos. (Ljósmyndasafn Reykjavíkur; 411 6390; www.photomuseum.is; 6th fl, Tryggvagata 15, Grófarhús; admission free; ☺noon-7pm Mon-Thu, to 6pm Fri, 1-5pm Sat & Sun)

Volcano House
MUSEUM

 8 Map p28, B1

This modern theatre with a hands-on lava exhibit in the foyer screens a 55-minute pair of films (hourly) about the Vestmannaeyjar volcanoes and Eyjafjallajökull. They show in German once daily in summer. (555 1900; www.volcanohouse.is; Tryggvagata 11; adult/child kr1990/free; ☺9am-10pm)

Understand
Icelandic Settlement & Sagas

Rumour, myth and fantastic tales of fierce storms and barbaric dog-headed people kept most explorers away from the great northern ocean, *oceanus innavigabilis*. Irish monks who regularly sailed to the Faroe Islands looking for seclusion were probably the first to stumble upon Iceland. It's thought that they settled around the year 700 but fled when Norsemen began to arrive in the early 9th century.

The Age of Settlement
The Age of Settlement is traditionally defined as between 870 and 930, when political strife on the Scandinavian mainland caused many to flee. Most North Atlantic Norse settlers were farmers and merchants who settled across Western Europe, marrying Britons, Westmen (Irish) and Scots.

Among Iceland's first Norse visitors was Norwegian Flóki Vilgerðarson, who uprooted his farm and headed for Snæland around 860. He navigated with ravens, which led him to his destination and provided his nickname, Hrafna-Flóki (Raven-Flóki). Hrafna-Flóki sailed to Vatnsfjörður on the west coast but became disenchanted with the conditions. On seeing the icebergs in the fjord he dubbed the country Ísland (Iceland) and returned to Norway. He did eventually settle in Iceland's Skagafjörður district.

According to the 12th-century *Íslendingabók* (a historical narrative of the Settlement Era), Ingólfur Arnarson fled Norway with his blood brother Hjörleifur, landing at Ingólfshöfði (southeast Iceland) in 871. They continued around the coast, and Ingólfur was then led to Reykjavík by a pagan ritual: he tossed his high-seat pillars (a symbol of authority) into the sea as they approached land. Wherever the gods brought the pillars ashore would be the settlers' new home. Ingólfur named Reykjavík (Smoky Bay) after the steam from its thermal springs. Hjörleifur settled near the present town of Vík, but was murdered by his slaves shortly thereafter.

The Saga Age
The Saga Age kicked off in the late 12th century, when the epic tales of the earlier 9th-to-10th-century settlement were recorded by historians and writers. These prose epics detail the family struggles, romance, vendettas and colourful characters of Settlement, and are the backbone of medieval Icelandic literature, and a rich source for historical understanding.

Dómkirkja
CHURCH

9 Map p28, C3

Iceland's main cathedral, Dómkirkja is a modest affair, but it played a vital role in the country's conversion to Lutheranism. The current building (built in the 18th century and enlarged in 1848) is small and perfectly proportioned, with a plain wooden interior animated by glints of gold. (www.domkirkjan.is; Kirkjustræti; ⊙10am-4.30pm Mon-Fri, Mass 11am Sun)

Nordic House
CULTURAL BUILDING

10 Map p28, B5

This cultural centre fosters connections between Iceland and its Nordic neighbours with a rich program of events, a library, an exhibition space (11am to 5pm) and a bistro. (Norræna Húsið; ☎551 7030; www.nordichouse.is; Sturlugata 5; ⊙9am-5pm Mon-Fri, 11am-5pm Sat; ⊒1, 3, 6, 12, 14)

Eating

Messinn
SEAFOOD $$

11 Map p28, D3

Make a beeline to Messinn for the best seafood that Reykjavík has to offer. The speciality is amazing pan-fries where your pick of fish is served up in a sizzling cast-iron skillet accompanied by buttery potatoes and salad. The mood is upbeat and comfortable, and the staff friendly. (☎546 0095; www.messinn.com; Lækjargata 6b; lunch mains

kr1900-2100, dinner mains kr2500-3800; ⊙11.30am-3pm & 5-10pm; ☎)

Apotek
FUSION $$$

12 Map p28, C2

This beautiful restaurant and bar with shining glass fixtures and a cool ambience is equally known for its delicious menu of small plates, perfect for sharing, and its top-flight cocktails. It's on the ground floor of the hotel of the same name. (☎551 0011; www.apotekrestaurant.is; Austurstræti 16; mains kr3000-8000; ⊙11.30am-1am)

Grillmarkaðurinn
FUSION $$$

13 Map p28, D2

Tippety-top dining is the order of the day here, from the moment you enter the glass atrium with the golden-globe lights to your first snazzy cocktail, and on through the meal. Service is impeccable, and locals and visitors alike rave about the food: locally sourced Icelan-

Local Life
The City's Best Hot Dogs
Icelanders swear the city's best hot dogs are at the **Bæjarins Beztu** (Map p28, D2; www.bbp.is; Tryggvagata; hot dogs kr420; ⊙10am-2am Sun-Thu, to 4.30am Fri & Sat; ⛴) truck near the harbour (patronised by Bill Clinton and late-night bar-hoppers). Use the vital sentence *Eina með öllu* ('One with everything') to get the quintessential favourite with sweet mustard, ketchup and crunchy onions.

dic ingredients prepared with culinary imagination by master chefs. (Grill Market; ☎571 7777; www.grillmarkadurinn. is; Lækargata 2a; mains kr4600-7000; ⊙11.30am-2pm Mon-Fri, 6-10.30pm Sun-Thu, to 11.30pm Fri & Sat)

Fiskfélagið   SEAFOOD $$$

 14 Map p28, C1

The 'Fish Company' takes Icelandic seafood recipes and spins them through a variety of far-flung inspirations from Fiji coconut to Spanish chorizo. Dine in an intimate-feeling stone-and-timber room with copper light fittings and quirky furnishings or out on the terrace. (☎552 5300; www.fishcompany.is; Vesturgata 2a; mains lunch kr2400-3000, dinner kr4900-6000; ⊙11.30am-2.30pm Mon-Sat, 5.30-11pm Sun-Thu, to 11.30pm Fri & Sat)

Stofan Kaffihús   CAFE $

15 Map p28, C1

This laid-back cafe in a historic brick building has a warm feel with its worn wooden floors, plump couches and spacious main room. Settle in for coffee, cake or soup, and watch the world go by. (☎546 1842; www.facebook.com/stofan.cafe/; Vesturgata 3; dishes kr1500-1600; ⊙9am-11pm Mon-Wed, to midnight Thu-Sat, 10am-10pm Sun; 🛜)

Fiskmarkaðurinn   SEAFOOD $$$

16 Map p28, B2

This restaurant excels in infusing Icelandic seafood and local produce

Jón Sigurðsson statue, Austurvöllur (p30)

with unique flavours like lotus root. The tasting menu (kr11,900) is tops, and it is renowned for its excellent sushi bar (kr3600 to kr4600). (Fishmarket; ☎578 8877; www.fiskmarkadurinn. is; Aðalstræti 12; mains kr5100-5700; ⊙6-11.30pm)

Bergsson Mathús   CAFE $$

 17 Map p28, C3

This popular, no-nonsense cafe features homemade breads, fresh produce and filling lunch specials. Stop by on weekends when locals flip through magazines, gossip and devour scrumptious brunch plates. After 4pm there is two-for-one takeaway. (☎571 1822;

www.bergsson.is; Templarasund 3; mains
kr2000-2400; ⏰7am-9pm Mon-Fri, to 5pm
Sat & Sun; 🖋)

Nora Magasin   BISTRO $$

 18 Map p28, C2

Hip and open plan, this buzzy bistro-
bar serves up a tasty selection of
pub food, from creative small plates
to burgers and fresh fish. Coffee
and cocktails run all night, but the
kitchen closes at 10pm or 11pm. (📞578
2010; Pósthússtræti 9; mains kr1700-2500;
⏰11.30am-1am Sun-Thu, to 3am Fri & Sat)

Icelandic Fish & Chips   SEAFOOD $$

Pick your fish, and voilà, spelt-batter
fried it becomes. Pair it with local
beer, organic salads (kr900) and
'Skyronnaises' – *skyr*-based sauces
(eg basil and garlic; kr290) that add a
zing to this most traditional of dishes.
It's located in the Volcano House
complex (see 8 ☻ Map p28, B1). (📞511 1118;
www.fishandchips.is; Tryggvagata 11; mains
kr1400-3000; ⏰11.30am-9pm Mon-Thu, to
10pm Fri-Sun)

Tapas Barinn   TAPAS $$$

A great place to hang with friends,
this outstanding tapas bar serves over
50 different dishes – thousands of
possible combinations! Alongside fa-
miliar Spanish nibbles, such as mixed
olives and *patatas bravas*, you'll find
Icelandic ingredients turned into tasty
titbits – saltfish or pan-fried lobster
tails. It neighbours the Stofan Kaffihús (see 15 ☻ Map p28, C1); book ahead

for a spot. (📞551 2344; www.tapas.is; Vesturgata 3b; tapas kr1600-2400; ⏰5-11.30pm
Sun-Thu, to 1am Fri & Sat)

Laundromat Café   INTERNATIONAL $$

This popular Danish import, downstairs from high-end cocktail bar
Loftið (see 22 ☻ Map p28, C2), attracts
both locals and travellers who devour
heaps of hearty mains in a cheery
environment surrounded by tattered
paperbacks. Go for the 'Dirty Breakfast' (kr2390) to sop up the previous
night's booze. Oh, and yes, there are
(busy) washers and dryers in the
basement (per wash/15-minute dry
kr750/750). Kids' play area, too. (www.
thelaundromatcafe.com; Austurstræti 9; mains
kr2000-2800; ⏰8am-11pm Sun-Wed, 9am-
midnight Thu-Sat; 🛜👨‍👧)

Lobster Hut   SEAFOOD $$

 19 Map p28, D2

What's it gonna be? Lobster soup? Lobster salad? Sandwich? This little food
truck dishes it all out, for fine diners
on the run. By day it's at Hlemmur Sq
and after 9pm it's on Lækergata in the
city centre. (mains kr1700-2500; ⏰11am-
2am Mon-Thu, to 6am Fri & Sat)

Drinking

Micro Bar   BAR

 20 Map p28, C1

Boutique brews is the name of the
game at this low-key spot in the heart
of the action. Bottles of beer represent

a slew of brands and countries, but more importantly you'll discover 10 local draughts on tap from the island's top microbreweries: one of the best selections in Reykjavík. Happy hour (5pm to 7pm) offers kr850 beers. (www.facebook.com/MicroBarIceland/; Vesturgata 2; ☾2pm-12.30am Sun-Thu, to 2am Fri & Sat)

Paloma
CLUB

21 🍷 Map p28, C1

One of Reykjavík's best late-night dance clubs, with DJs upstairs laying down reggae, electronica and pop, and a dark deep house dance scene in the basement. (www.facebook.com/BarPaloma/; Naustin 1-3; ☾8pm-1am Thu & Sun, to 4.30am Fri & Sat; 🏳️‍🌈)

Loftið
COCKTAIL BAR

22 🍷 Map p28, C2

Dress up to join the fray at this airy upstairs lounge with a zinc bar, retro tailor-shop-inspired decor, vintage tiles and a swank, older crowd. The well booze here is the top-shelf liquor elsewhere, and jazzy bands play from time to time. (☎551 9400; www.loftidbar.is; 2nd fl, Austurstræti 9; ☾2pm-1am Sun-Thu, 4pm-3am Fri & Sat)

Skúli Craft Bar
CRAFT BEER

23 🍷 Map p28, C2

Loads of draught and bottled beers (130 at last count) served with a smile in a welcoming brick and beam

---

Icelandic Pop

Iceland's pop-music scene is one of its great gifts to the world. Internationally famous Icelandic musicians include (of course) Björk and her former band, the Sugarcubes. Sigur Rós followed Björk to stardom; their concert movie *Heima* (2007) is a must-see. Indie-folk Of Monsters and Men stormed the US charts in 2011 with *My Head Is an Animal;* their latest album is *Beneath the Skin* (2015). Ásgeir had a breakout hit with *In the Silence* (2014).

Reykjavík's flourishing music landscape is constantly changing – visit www.icelandmusic.is and www.grapevine.is for news and listings. Just a few examples of local groups include Seabear, an indie-folk band, which spawned top acts like Sin Fang (*Flowers;* 2013) and Sóley (*We Sink;* 2012). Árstíðir record minimalist indie-folk, and released *Verloren Verleden* with Anneke van Giersbergen in 2016.

Other local bands include GusGus, a pop-electronica act, FM Belfast (electronica) and múm (experimental electronica mixed with traditional instruments). Or check out Singapore Sling for straight-up rock and roll. If your visit coincides with one of Iceland's many music festivals, go!

sort of place. Six-beer flight costs kr3100. (☏519 6455; Aðalstræti 9; ⏱2-11pm Sun-Thu, to 1am Fri & Sat)

Frederiksen Ale House PUB

24 Map p28, C2

A modest selection of draught beers (happy hour is two-for-one; 4pm to 7pm) meets lots of bottled offerings and a good pub food menu, including brunch. (☏571 0055; www.frederiksen.is; Hafnarstræti 5)

Sæta Svínið Gastropub PUB

25 Map p28, C2

Tuck into creative pub food while quaffing a litre of the local ale at this three-storey new entry on Reykjavík's gastropub scene. (www.saetasvinid.is; Hafnarstræti 1; ⏱11.30am-11.30pm)

Hressingarskálinn PUB

26 Map p28, D2

Known as Hressó, this large cafe-bar serves a diverse menu until 10pm – everything from porridge to *plokkfiskur* (fish stew); mains kr2800 to kr5000 – then at weekends it loses its civilised veneer and concentrates on drinks and dancing for the younger set. (Hressó; www.hresso.is; Austurstræti 20; ⏱9am-1am Sun-Thu, 10am-4.30am Fri & Sat; 🛜)

English Pub PUB

27 Map p28, C2

Reliable pub for catching football matches. (Enski Barinn; www.enskibarinn.

is; Austurstræti 12a; ⏱noon-1am Sun-Thu, to 4.30am Fri & Sat)

Ölsmiðjan BAR

28 Map p28, C3

An Icelandic dive bar with low beer prices and decent ambience. (Lækjargata 10; ⏱3pm-1am)

Græna Herbergið CLUB

29 Map p28, D2

DJs and live music alternate in this large, two-storey bar. (www.greenroom.is; Lækjargata 6; ⏱4pm-1am Tue-Thu & Sun, to 3am Fri & Sat)

Entertainment

Húrra LIVE MUSIC

30 ⭐ Map p28, C1

Dark and raw, this large bar opens up its back room to make a concert venue, with live music or DJs most nights, and is one of the best places in town to close out the night. Run by the same folks as Bravó (p62), it's got a range of beers on tap and happy hour runs till 9pm (beer or wine kr700). (Tryggvagata 22; ⏱5pm-1am Sun-Thu, to 4.30am Fri & Sat; 🛜)

Gaukurinn LIVE MUSIC

Grungy and glorious, it's a solid stop for live music, comedy, karaoke and open mikes. Happy hour is 7pm to 10pm (beer/wine kr600/750). The bar is in the same building as Húrra (see

30 Map p28, C1). (www.gaukurinn.is; Tryggvagata 22; from 2pm daily)

Iðnó Theatre

THEATRE

31 Map p28, C3

Music and Icelandic theatre, tending towards the comedic. (562 9700; www.idno.is; Vonarstræti 3)

Shopping

Kirsuberjatréð

ARTS & CRAFTS

32 Map p28, B1

This women's art-and-design collective in an interesting 1882 former bookshop sells weird and wonderful fish-skin handbags, music boxes made from string, and, our favourite, beautiful coloured bowls made from radish slices. It's been around for 25 years and now has 11 designers. (Cherry Tree; 562 8990; www.kirs.is; Vesturgata 4; 10am-7pm & 8-10pm Mon-Fri, to 5pm Sat, to 4pm Sun)

Eymundsson

BOOKS

33 Map p28, D2

This big central bookshop has a superb choice of English-language books, newspapers, magazines and maps, along with a great cafe. A second branch can be found at Skólavörðustígur 11. (www.eymundsson.is; Austurstræti 18; 9am-10pm Mon-Fri, 10am-10pm Sat & Sun;)

Local Life

Kolaportið Flea Market

Held in a huge industrial building by the harbour, the weekend **Kolaportið Flea Market** (Map p28, C1; www.kolaportid.is; Tryggvagata 19; 11am-5pm Sat & Sun) is a Reykjavík institution. There's a huge tumble of second-hand clothes and old toys, plus cheap imports. There's also a food section that sells traditional eats like *rúgbrauð* (geothermally baked rye bread), *brauðterta* ('sandwich cake', a layering of bread with mayonnaise-based fillings) and *hákarl* (fermented shark).

Kogga

CERAMICS

34 Map p28, B1

This tiny ceramic studio in the lower level of an old Reykjavík house offers imaginative pottery. (552 6036; www.kogga.is; Vesturgata 5; 9am-6pm Mon-Fri, 11am-3pm Sat)

Kickstart

CLOTHING

35 Map p28, B1

This tiny but inviting men's store stocks ties, gloves, motorcycle gear and other manly accoutrements. (568 0809; www.kickstart.is; Vesturgata 12; noon-6pm Mon-Fri)

Explore

Old Harbour

Largely a service harbour until recently, the Old Harbour and the adjacent Grandi (Örfirisey) neigbourhood have blossomed into a hot spot for tourists, with several museums, volcano and Northern Lights films, and interesting eateries and shops. Whale-watching and puffin-viewing trips depart from the pier and photo ops abound with views of the Harpa concert hall and snowcapped mountains beyond.

The Sights in a Day

☀ Start your day with some contemporary Icelandic art at **Kling & Bang** (p42) and **Nýló** (p43). Have lunch at one of the area's good, casual restaurants, from **Bryggjan Brugghús** (p44), to the **Fish & Chips** (p44) or **Walk the Plank** (p45) seafood trolleys, excellent, rustic seafood joint **Sægreifinn** (p44) or hamburger hangout **Hamborgara Búllan** (p44).

☼ Then hit the museum of your choice: **Víkin Maritime Museum** (p41) for nautical history, the **Saga Museum** (p41) for bloodthirsty saga simulations, **Aurora Reykjavík** (p43) for a recreation of the grand borealis, or **Whales of Iceland** (p42) for life-size reconstructions of the great beasts you spotted in the morning. The **Cinema at Old Harbour Village No 2** (p43) is perfect for catching Icelandic nature films about volcanoes and Northern Lights. And **Omnom Chocolate** (p42) offers factory tours. An ice cream at **Valdi's** (p43) will give you a second wind.

☾ Stroll the sparkling water, taking in the views back to Harpa and Hallgrímskirkja. Then dine at **Matur og Drykkur** (p43) or **Forréttabarinn** (p44) and have cocktails at chic **Slippbarinn** (p47).

 Best of Reykjavík

Cafes & Bars

Slippbarinn (p47)

Café Haiti (p47)

With Kids

Saga Museum (p41)

Whales of Iceland (p42)

Omnom Chocolate (p42)

Aurora Reykjavík (p43)

Valdi's (p43)

Getting There

🚌 **Bus** Bus 14 runs all the way across town: from Laugardalur park to Hlemmur, BSÍ bus terminal, the National Museum, Old Reykjavík and finally the Old Harbour. The Mýrargata stop is nearest for whale-watching outfits, while Grandagarður is closest to the Víkin Maritime Museum and other sights.

🚶 **On Foot** You can walk to the Old Harbour.

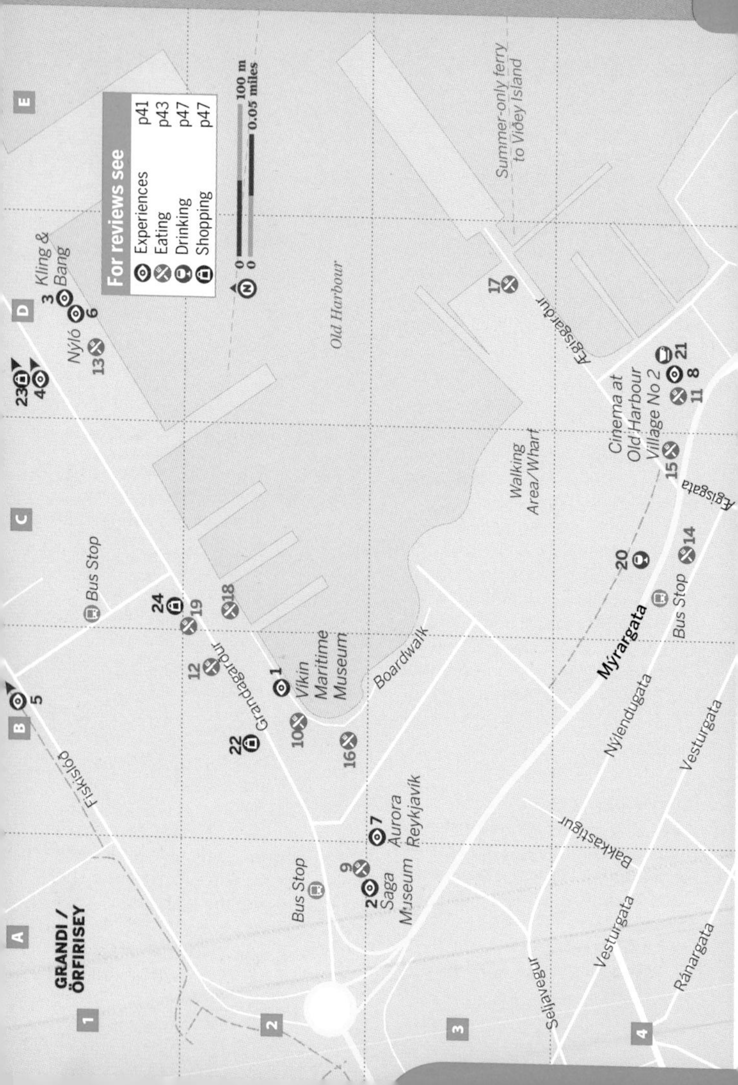

For reviews see
Experiences p41
Eating p43
Drinking p47
Shopping p47
0 100 m
0 0.05 miles
GRANDI / ÖRFIRISEY
A
B
C
D
E
1
2
3
4
Kling & Bang
Nýló
Old Harbour
Summer-only ferry to Viðey Island
Ægisgarður
Cinema at Old Harbour Village No 2
Walking Area/Wharf
Ægisgata
Mýrargata
Bus Stop
Bus Stop
Bus Stop
Grandagarður
Víkin Maritime Museum
Boardwalk
Fiskislóð
Aurora Reykjavík
Saga Museum
Nýlendugata
Vesturgata
Bakkastígur
Seljavegur
Vesturgata
Ránargata

Recreation of the Battle of Orlygsstathir, Saga Museum

Experiences

Víkin Maritime Museum MUSEUM

1 🎯 Map p40, B2

Based appropriately in a former fish-freezing plant, this museum celebrates the country's seafaring heritage, focusing on the trawlers that transformed Iceland's economy. Guided tours go aboard coastguard ship *Óðínn* (kr1200, or joint ticket with museum kr2200; check website for times). The boat is a veteran of the 1970s Cod Wars, when British and Icelandic fishermen came to blows over fishing rights in the North Atlantic. (Víkin Sjóminjasafnið; ☎517 9400; www. maritimemuseum.is; Grandagarður 8; adult/child kr1500/free; ⏰10am-5pm; 🚌14)

Saga Museum MUSEUM

2 🎯 Map p40, A3

The endearingly bloodthirsty Saga Museum is where Icelandic history is brought to life by eerie silicon models and a multilanguage soundtrack with thudding axes and hair-raising screams. Don't be surprised if you see some of the characters wandering around town, as moulds were taken from Reykjavík residents (the owner's daughters are the Irish princess and the little slave gnawing a fish!). (☎511 1517; www.sagamuseum.is; Grandagarður 2; adult/child kr2100/800; ⏰10am-6pm; 🚌14)

Whales of Iceland

Kling & Bang · GALLERY

3 ⊙ Map p40, D1

This perennially cutting-edge artist-run exhibition space is a favourite with locals, and now has a new expanded gallery in the renovated Marshall House in the Grandi area near the Old Harbour. (✐691 4243; http://this.is/kling andbang/; Grandagarður 20, Marshall Húsið, Grandi; admission free; ⊘2-6pm Thu-Sun)

Omnom Chocolate · FACTORY

4 ⊙ Map p40, D1

Reserve ahead for a tour at this full-service chocolate factory where you'll see how cocoa beans are transformed into high-end scrumptious delights. The shop also sells its bonbons and stylish bars, with specially designed labels and myriad sophisticated flavours. You'll also find the bars in shops throughout Iceland. (✐519 5959; www.omnomchoc olate.com; Hólmaslóð 4, Grandi; adult/child kr3000/1500; ⊘8am-5pm Mon-Fri)

Whales of Iceland · MUSEUM

5 ⊙ Map p40, B1

Ever stroll beneath a blue whale? This museum houses full-sized models of the 23 whales found off Iceland's coast. The largest museum of this type in Europe, it also displays models of whale skeletons, and has good audio guides and multimedia screens to explain what you're seeing. It has a cafe and gift shop, online ticket discounts and family tickets (kr5800). (📞571 0077; www.whalesoficeland.is; Fiskislóð 23-25; adult/child kr2900/1500; ⏰10am-6pm Jun-Aug, to 5pm Sep-May; 🚌14)

Nýló
GALLERY

 6 ◉ Map p40, D1

This dynamic centre for emerging and established contemporary artists, live music and other performances has a brand-new space in the renovated Marshall House in the Grandi neighbourhood near the Old Harbour. (Nýlistasafnið – The Living Art Museum; 📞551 4350; www.nylo.is; Grandagarður 20, Marshall Húsið, Grandi; admission free; ⏰10am-6pm Tue-Fri, to 9pm Thu, noon-5pm Sat & Sun)

Aurora Reykjavík
EXHIBITION

7 ◉ Map p40, B3

Learn about the classical tales explaining the Northern Lights, then watch a 35-minute surround-sound panoramic HD recreation of Icelandic auroras. (Northern Lights Centre; 📞780 4500; www.aurorareykjavik.is; Grandagarður 2; adult/child kr1600/1000; ⏰9am-9pm; 🚌14)

Cinema at Old Harbour Village No 2
CINEMA

8 ◉ Map p40, D4

A tiny theatre perches in the top of one of the rehabbed Old Harbour warehouses. Nature films include volcanoes

(Eyjafjallajökull, Westmann Islands), the creation of Iceland, and the Northern Lights, and are mostly shown in English with occasional German screenings. See schedule online. (📞898 6628; www.thecinema.is; Geirsgata 7b; adult/child kr1800/900; 🚌1, 3, 6, 11, 12, 13, 14)

Eating

Matur og Drykkur
ICELANDIC $$

 9 🍴 Map p40, A2

One of Reykjavík's top high-concept restaurants, Matur og Drykkur means 'food and drink', and you surely will be plied with the best of both. The brainchild of brilliant chef Gísli Matthías Auðunsson, who also owns the excellent Slippurinn (p102) in the Vestmannaeyjar islands, creates inventive versions of traditional Icelandic fare. Book ahead in high season and for dinner. (📞571 8877; www.maturogdrykkur.is; Grandagarður 2; lunch mains kr1900-3200, dinner menus kr3000-5000; ⏰11.30am-3pm Mon-Sat, 6-10.30pm Tue-Sat; 🚌14)

 Local Life

Ice Cream!

Happy families flock to iconic **Valdi's** (Map p40, C1; 📞586 8088; www.valdis.is; Grandagarður 21; scoops kr450; ⏰11.30am-11pm May-Aug; 👶) throughout summer. Join the crush waiting to choose a scoop from the huge array of homemade ice creams. Totally casual, totally fun.

Bryggjan Brugghús

BREWPUB $$

10 Map p40, B2

This enormous, golden-lit microbrewery and bistro is a welcome respite for one of its home-brewed beers (start with IPA, lager and seasonal beers, from 12 taps) or for an extensive menu of seafood and meat dishes, and occasional DJs. (456 4040; www.bryggjanbrugghus.is; Grandagarður 8; mains kr2300-5000; 11am-midnight Sun-Thu, to 1am Sat & Sun, kitchen 11.30am-11pm;)

Sægreifinn

SEAFOOD $

11 Map p40, D4

Sidle into this green harbourside shack for the most famous lobster soup (kr1350) in the capital, or to choose from a fridge full of fresh fish skewers to be grilled on the spot. Though the original sea baron sold the restaurant some years ago, the place retains a homey, laid-back feel. (Seabaron; 553 1500; www.saegreifinn.is; Geirsgata 8; mains kr1350-1900; 11.30am-11pm mid-May–Aug, to 10pm Sep–mid-May)

Coocoo's Nest

CAFE $$

12 Map p40, B2

Pop into this cool eatery tucked behind the Old Harbour for popular weekend brunches (dishes kr1700 to kr2200; 11am to 4pm Friday to Sunday) paired with decadent cocktails (kr1300). The menu changes and there are nightly themes, but it's always scrumptious. (552 5454; www.coocoosnest.is; Grandagarður 23; mains kr1700-4500; 11am-10pm Tue-Sat, to 4pm Sun;)

Bergsson RE

SEAFOOD $$

13 Map p40, D1

This long-time restaurant-operating family (they operate the Bergsson Mathús; p33) has opened this new spot in the Grandi neighbourhood. It's got great harbour views and the lunch menu changes daily, but always features the freshest catch. (571 0822; www.bergsson.net; Grandagarður 16; mains kr1400-2400; 9am-5pm Mon-Fri; 14)

Forréttabarinn

TAPAS $$

14 Map p40, C4

Tapas restaurants are popular in the capital, and this hip joint near the harbour is a favourite for its menu of creative plates such as cod and pork belly with white beans. There is also an airy and relaxed bar area. (Starter Bar; 517 1800; www.forrettabarinn.is; Nýlendugata 14, entrance from Mýrargata; plates kr1700-2600; 4-10pm, bar to 11pm;)

Hamborgara Búllan

BURGERS $

15 Map p40, C4

The Old Harbour's outpost of burgerdom and Americana proffers savoury patties that are perennial local favourites. Russell Crowe was spotted here while filming in 2012. (Hamborgarabúlla Tómasar; 511 1888; www.bullan.is; Geirsgata 1; mains kr1200-1800; 11.30am-9pm;)

Fish & Chips

SEAFOOD $

16 Map p40, B2

Delicious, piping hot fish and chips are on offer at this food truck near the

Understand
Eating the Locals

Many restaurants and tour operators in Iceland tout their more unusual delicacies: whale (*hvál/hvalur*), shark (fermented and called *hákarl*) and puffin (*lundi*). Before you dig in, consider that what may have been sustainable with 332,000 Icelanders becomes taxing on species and delicate ecosystems when 1,300,000 tourists annually get involved. Be aware:

While we do not exclude restaurants that serve these meats from our listings, you can opt not to order the meat, or easily find whale-free spots at www.icewhale.is/whale-friendly-restaurants.

▶ An estimated 40% to 60% of whale meat consumption is by tourists.

▶ A total of 82% of Icelanders never eat whale meat.

▶ Only 3% of Icelanders eat whale regularly.

▶ Between 75% and 85% of minke whale is thrown away after killing.

▶ Fin whales are classified as endangered globally; their status in the North Atlantic is hotly debated.

▶ Iceland's Ministry of Industries and Innovation maintains the whale catch is sustainable, at less than 1% of local stock, despite international protest.

▶ The Greenland shark, which is used for *hákarl*, has a conservation status of 'near threatened' globally.

▶ In 2002 there were an estimated seven million puffins in Iceland, in 2015 there were about four million – a 43% drop, with much more among juveniles (–65%) due to consistently poor chick production.

▶ At the time of writing, Icelandic puffins were experiencing an enormous breeding failure in their largest colonies, in the Vestmannaeyjar islands.

Vikín Maritime Museum. (Old Harbour; mains kr1200-2000; ☺11am-9pm; ◻14)

Walk the Plank   SEAFOOD $
17 🍴 Map p40, D3

On decent-weather days and around whale-watching departures, this tiny food truck opens its window and dishes up yummy crab-cake sliders on the quay. (ww.facebook.com/walktheplank iceland/; Ægisgarður; mains kr1500-1900; ☺10am-8pm)

Understand

Partying in Reykjavík

Reykjavík's renowned *djammið* is the lively surge of drinkers and party-ers through central Reykjavík's streets, pubs and dance clubs. Thanks to the high price of alcohol, things generally don't get going until late. Icelanders brave the melee at government alcohol store **Vínbúðin** (www. vinbudin.is; Austurstræti 10a; ☉11am-6pm Mon-Thu & Sat, to 7pm Fri), then toddle home for a prebup party before hitting the streets.

The action is concentrated near Laugavegur and Austurstræti. Places stay open until 1am Sunday to Thursday (4am or 5am on Friday and Saturday). You'll pay kr1000 to kr1600 per pint of beer, and cocktails are kr1800 to kr2700. Some venues have cover charges (about kr1000) after midnight; many have early happy hours saving kr500 to kr700 per beer. Download smartphone app *Reykjavík Appy Hour*, and check Grape-vine (www.grapevine.is) for the latest listings.

Local Liquors

Check out **Brennivín** (http://brennivin.com), a neon-green, caraway-flavoured 'black death' schnapps; **Opal**, a flavoured vodka in several menthol and liquorice varieties; **Flóki Whisky** (www.flokiwhisky.is), an Icelandic single malt whisky; the **64° Reykjavík Distillery** (www.reykja vikdistillery.is), a microdistillery producing Katla vodka, aquavit, herbal liqueurs and schnapps; and **Reyka Vodka** (www.reyka.com), Iceland's first distillery, in Borgarnes.

Beer!

Egils, Gull, Thule and Viking are the most common beers (typically lagers) in Iceland, but craft breweries have taken the scene by storm. Try **Borg Brugghús** (www.borgbrugghus.is), an award-winning craft brewery with beers from Brió pilsner to Garún stout; **Einstök Brewing Company** (www. einstokbeer.com), an Akureyri-based craft brewery with a distinctive Icelandic Pale Ale, among other ales and porters; **Bruggsmiðjan–Kaldi** (www.bruggsmidjan.is), which is produced using Czech techniques, and has a dedicated bar in Reykjavík; **Steðji Brugghús** (www.stedji.com), a brewhouse offering lager and seasonal beers; and **Ölvisholt Brugghús** (www.brugghus.is) with microbrews from South Iceland, including eye-catching Lava beer. **Bryggjan Brugghús** (www.bryggjanbrugghus.is) has a microbrewery at Reykjavík's Old Harbour.

Kaffivagninn
DINER $$

18 🚋 Map p40, C2

This harbourside eatery has broad windows looking onto the bobbing boats, and serves good breakfasts and hearty seafood-based lunches. (☑551 5932; www.kaffivagninn.is; Grandagarður 10; mains kr2300-2700; ⊙7.30am-6pm Mon-Fri, from 9.30am Sat & Sun; 🛜)

Burið
CHEESE $

19 🚋 Map p40, C2

Select from a broad range of Icelandic cheeses and *skyr* (yoghurt-like dessert), and other deli and sweet treats. (☑551 8400; http://blog.burid.is; Grandagarður 35; ⊙11am-6pm Mon-Fri, noon-5pm Sat; 🚌14)

Drinking

Slippbarinn
COCKTAIL BAR

20 🍺 Map p40, C4

Jetsetters unite at this buzzy restaurant (mains kr2900 to kr5000) and bar at the Old Harbour in the **Icelandair Hotel Reykjavík Marina**. It's bedecked with vintage record players and chatting fans sipping some of the best cocktails in town. (☑560 8080; www.slippbarinn.is; Mýrargata 2; ⊙noon-midnight Sun-Thu, to 1am Fri & Sat; 🛜)

Café Haiti
CAFE

21 🍺 Map p40, D4

If you're a coffee aficionado, this tiny cafe in the Old Harbour is the place for you. Owner Elda buys her beans from her home country Haiti, and roasts and grinds them on-site, producing what regulars swear are the best cups of coffee in the whole country. (☑588 8484; www.cafehaiti.is; Geirsgata 7c; ⊙8am-10pm Sun-Thu, to midnight Fri & Sat)

Shopping

Steinunn
CLOTHING

22 🔒 Map p40, B2

Browse the couture collection of celebrated Icelandic designer Steinunn Sigurðardóttir featuring innovative knitwear. (☑588 6649; www.steinunn.com; Grandagarður 17; ⊙11am-6pm Mon-Fri, 1-4pm Sat)

Farmers Market
CLOTHING

23 🔒 Map p40, D1

This design company run by a local couple is not about food, but rather sustainably designed and created clothing, accessories and housewares with an emphasis on natural fabrics and materials. (☑552 1960; www.farmersmarket.is; Hólmaslóð 2; ⊙10am-6pm Mon-Fri, 11am-4pm Sat, noon-4pm Sun)

Krínolín
CLOTHING

24 🔒 Map p40, C1

Sigrún Einarsdóttir creates clothing out of natural fabrics like wool, lambskin and fish skin. (www.krinolin.is; Grandagarður 37)

Laugavegur & Skólavörðustígur

Reykjavík's main street for shopping and people-watching is bustling Laugavegur. The narrow, one-way lane and its side streets blossom with the capital's most interesting shops, cafes and bars. At its western end, its name changes to Bankastræti, then Austurstræti. Running up-hill off Bankastræti, artists' street Skólavörðustígur ends at spectacular modernist church, Hallgrímskirkja.

The Sights in a Day

Breakfast at **Grái Kötturinn** (p59) then stroll across the street to the fascinating **Culture House** (p55). Next be dazzled by the gorgeous interior of **Harpa** (p55), before choosing among the neighbourhood's many museums. Hit the **Icelandic Phallological Museum** (p56) to see coolly curated penises before perusing top art at the **Reykjavík Art Museum – Kjarvalsstaðir** (p56) or at either of the (other) Jónsson museums: **Ásgrímur Jónsson Collection** (p57) or **Einar Jónsson Museum** (p57).

Get a bite to eat at delicious, organic **Gló** (p58), then zip to the top of **Hallgrímskirkja** (p50) for views. If you're up for more art, head over to the excellent **National Gallery of Iceland** (p56), by the lake. If you'd rather unwind, take a dip in the geothermal pools at the classic **Sundhöllin** (p57).

Be sure to reserve ahead for any of the area's top restaurants, which are some of the best in the country: **Dill** (p58), **Snaps** (p58), or **Þrír Frakkar** (p59). Or kick off a late-night *djammið* party blow-out with casual eats at lively **Vegamót** (p60) or **Public House** (p60), or seafood at **Ostabúðin** (p59). Quieter night? Take in an Icelandic flick at **Bíó Paradís** (p64).

For a local's day in Laugavegur & Skólavörðustígur, see p52.

 Top Experiences

Hallgrímskirkja (p50)

 Local Life

Djammið Nightlife (p52)

♥ **Best of Reykjavík**

Eating

Dill (p58)

Þrír Frakkar (p59)

Bakarí Sandholt (p60)

Grái Kötturinn (p59)

Hverfisgata 12 (p61)

Shopping

Kiosk (p65)

Kraum (p64)

KronKron (p66)

Skúmaskot (p65)

Handknitting Association of Iceland (p66)

Getting There

⊕ On Foot Within the neighbourhood it's easiest to walk, as many of the roads are one-way or pedestrianised.

🚍 Bus Buses 1, 3, 6, 11, 12 and 13 run between the Hlemmur at the eastern end of Laugavegur, along the waterfront to Lækjartorg Sq, before continuing onward.

Top Experiences
Hallgrímskirkja

Reykjavík's soaring white-concrete church dominates the city skyline, and is visible from 20km away. The graceful church was named after poet Reverend Hallgrímur Pétursson (1614–74), who wrote Iceland's most popular hymn book, *Passion Hymns*. The church's size and radical design caused controversy, and its architect, Guðjón Samúelsson (1887–1950), never saw its completion – it took 41 years (1945–86) to build.

⊙ Map p54, C4

☎ 510 1000

www.hallgrimskirkja.is

Skólavörðustígur

tower adult/child kr900/100

🕙 9am-9pm Jun-Sep, to 5pm Oct-May

Facade & Tower

The columns on either side of the church's signature 74.5m-high tower represent volcanic basalt, part of architect Guðjón Samúelsson's desire to create a national architectural style. Get a spectacular panorama of the city by taking an elevator trip up the dizzying tower, where you'll find great photo ops from the viewing area.

Organ

In contrast to the high drama outside, the Lutheran church's interior is quite plain. The most eye-catching feature is the vast, gleaming 5275-pipe organ, installed in 1992. It was made in Germany by Johannes Klais Orgelbau and individuals sponsored each of the pipes; their names are inscribed on them. Towards the altar, you'll find the quaint older organ, still in use.

Concerts & Services

From mid-June to mid-August, hear half-hour **choral concerts** (www.scholacantorum.is; admission kr2000) at noon on Wednesday, and **organ recitals** (www.listvinafelag.is) at noon on Saturday and some Thursdays (admission kr2000), and for one hour on Sunday at 5pm (admission kr2500). **Services** are held Sunday at 11am, with a small service Wednesday at 8am. There is an English service on the last Sunday of the month at 2pm.

Leifur Eiríksson Statue

At the front, gazing proudly into the distance, is a statue of the Viking Leifur Eiríksson, the first European to discover America. A present from the USA on the 1000th anniversary of the Alþingi (parliament) in 1930, it was designed by Alexander Stirling Calder (1870–1945), the father of the perhaps more famous, modern mobilist and sculptor Alexander Calder (1898–1976).

☑ **Top Tips**

▶ Try for a local's pronunciation: Hallgrímskirkja is pronounced *hatl-krims-kirk-ya*.

▶ There are occasional rotating art exhibitions in the church's foyer.

▶ Check online for the schedule of organ and choral recitals during your visit.

✕ **Take a Break**

Cross the street to **ROK** (Map p54, C3; ☎544 4443; www.rokrestaurant.is; Frakkstígur 26a; dishes kr1400-1700; ⏱11.30am-11pm) for small tapas-style plates of Icelandic fare.

Head down Skólavörðustígur to a plethora of eateries; try classic Kaffi Mokka (p62), one of Reykjavík's first coffee shops, for a light meal.

Local Life
Djammið Nightlife

Reykjavík is renowned for its wild, wonderful party scene. Called *djammið* (meaning going out on the town), the high-spirited nightlife is at its roaringest on weekends: many cafes and bistros transform into raucous beer-soaked bars, joining the dedicated pubs and clubs. But it's not the quantity of drinking dens that makes Reykjavík's nightlife special – it's the crowd's upbeat energy.

❶ Warming Up

As any good pub crawler knows, you gotta warm up so you don't break something. Start the night at **Kaldi** (www.kaldibar.is; Laugavegur 20b; ⊙noon-1am Sun-Thu, to 3am Fri & Sat) while you're still in the mood to discern quality beer. Effortlessly cool with mismatched seats and teal banquettes, plus a popular smoking courtyard, Kaldi carries the full range of its own microbrews, not available

elsewhere. A piano is available for anyone to play.

2 The Beautiful People

The old house with the London Underground symbol over the door contains one of Reykjavík's coolest bars: **Kaffibarinn** (www.kaffibarinn.is; Bergstaðastræti 1; ⏰3pm-1am Sun-Thu, to 4.30am Fri & Sat; 🛜). It had a starring role in the cult movie *101 Reykjavík* (2000), and at weekends you may need a famous face or a battering ram to get in, it's so packed.

3 Cool Cats

If you couldn't get into Kaffibarinn, or you're just ready to move on, head down to cool, arty **Boston** (www.facebook.com/boston.reykjavik/; Laugavegur 28b; ⏰4pm-1am Sun-Thu, to 3am Fri & Sat). You'll find it up through a doorway on Laugavegur that leads to this laid-back lounge where hip locals hang, and where DJs spin from time to time.

4 Rock Out!

Or, go next door for beer, beards and the odd flying bottle...atmospheric **Dillon** (☎578 2424; Laugavegur 30; ⏰2pm-1am Sun-Thu, to 3am Fri & Sat) is a RRRRROCK pub with a great beer garden. Frequent loud, live bands hit its tiny corner stage. Get dark and get sweaty.

5 The Shank of the Evening

By now you should be feeling the *djammið* vibe; it's a perfect time to simply stroll along packed Laugavegur, people-watching and striking up conversations. This may be the moment where you toss guidebook routes and just roll with the locals: pubs and late-night dives abound throughout the centre.

6 Time to Dance

Ostensibly a queer bar, **Kiki** (www.kiki.is; Laugavegur 22; ⏰9pm-1am Thu, to 4.30am Fri & Sat) is also the place to go get your dance on, since much of Reykjavík's nightlife centres around the booze, not the groove. It's only open Thursday to Saturday, but if you can squeeze beneath the flamingo sign and beyond the rainbow-striped tin siding, you'll find one of Reykjavík's best dance parties.

7 Staggering Home

The atmosphere at one of Reykjavík's oldest joints, **Prikið** (☎551 2866; www.prikid.is; Bankastræti 12; ⏰8am-1am Mon-Thu, to 4.30am Fri, 11am-4.30am Sat, 11am-midnight Sun), falls somewhere between diner and saloon, though it usually gets dancey in the wee hours. If you're still standing and you're longing for some greasy eats before heading home, join the locals tucking into burgers or the popular next-day 'hangover killer' breakfast. Or grab a great freshly made pizza slice at **The Deli** (www.deli.is; Bankastræti 14; slices kr500; ⏰10am-9pm Mon-Wed, 11am-5am or 6am Thu-Sat), just up the block.

NORTH ATLANTIC OCEAN

Old Harbour

Harpa

Hlemmur Bus Terminal

Laugavegur

Icelandic Phallological Museum

Sundhöllin

Hallgrímskirkja

Einar Jónsson Museum

Ásgrímur Jónsson Collection

National Gallery of Iceland

Culture House

EDDIE CHUI / 500PX ©

Harpa

Experiences

Harpa
CULTURAL BUILDING

1  Map p54, B1

With its ever-changing facets glistening on the water's edge, Reykjavík's
sparkling Harpa concert hall and
cultural centre is a beauty to behold.
In addition to a season of top-notch
shows (some free), it's worth stopping by to explore the shimmering
interior with harbour vistas, or take
a 45-minute **tour** of the hall (kr1950;
⏰11am, 1.30pm, 3.30pm & 5.30pm daily mid-
May–mid-September, 3.30pm Mon-Fri, 11am
& 3.30pm Sat & Sun rest of year). (📞box
office 528 5050; www.harpa.is; Austurbakki 2;
⏰8am-midnight, box office 10am-6pm)

Culture House
ART MUSEUM

2  Map p54, B2

This fantastic collaboration between
the National Museum, National
Gallery and four other organisations
creates a superbly curated exhibition
covering the artistic and cultural
heritage of Iceland from Settlement
to today. Priceless artefacts are
arranged by theme, and highlights
include 14th-century manuscripts,
contemporary art and items including the skeleton of a great auk (now
extinct). The renovated 1908 building
is beautiful, with great views of the
harbour, and a cafe on the ground
floor. Check website for free guided
tours. (Þjóðmenningarhúsið; 📞530 2210;

www.culturehouse.is; Hverfisgata 15; adult/
child kr1200/free; ⊙10am-5pm May–mid-
Sep, closed Mon mid-Sep–Apr)

National Gallery of Iceland

MUSEUM

3 ◉ Map p54, A3

This pretty stack of marble atriums
and spacious galleries overlooking
Tjörnin offers ever-changing exhibits
drawn from the 10,000-piece collection. The museum can only exhibit
a small sample at any time; shows
range from 19th- and 20th-century
paintings by Iceland's favourite sons
and daughters (including Jóhannes
Kjarval and Nína Sæmundsson) to
sculptures by Sigurjón Ólafsson and
others. The museum ticket also covers entry to the Ásgrímur Jónsson
Collection (p57) and Sigurjón Ólafsson Museum (p69). (Listasafn Íslands;
☑515 9600; www.listasafn.is; Fríkirkjuvegur
7; adult/child kr1500/free; ⊙10am-5pm
mid-May–mid-Sep, 11am-5pm Tue-Sun mid-
Sep–mid-May)

Top Tip

Three for the Price of One

▶ The Reykjavík Art Museum ticket
covers all three of its sites.

▶ The National Gallery ticket is also
good at the nearby Ásgrímur Jónsson Collection, and further afield
Sigurjón Ólafsson Museum.

Icelandic Phallological Museum

MUSEUM

4 ◉ Map p54, E4

Oh, the jokes are endless here, but
though this unique museum houses
a huge collection of penises, it's
actually very well done. From pickled
pickles to petrified wood, there are
286 different members on display,
representing all Icelandic mammals
and beyond. Featured items include
contributions from sperm whales
and a polar bear, minuscule mouse
bits, silver castings of each member
of the Icelandic handball team and a
single human sample – from deceased
mountaineer Páll Arason. (Hið Íslenzka
Reðasafn; ☑561 6663; www.phallus.is;
Laugavegur 116; adult/child kr1250/free;
⊙10am-6pm)

Reykjavík Art Museum – Kjarvalsstaðir

ART MUSEUM

5 ◉ Map p54, E4

The angular glass-and-wood
Kjarvalsstaðir, which looks out
onto **Miklatún Park**, is named for
Jóhannes Kjarval (1885–1972), one
of Iceland's most popular classical
artists. He was a fisherman until his
crew paid for him to study at the
Academy of Fine Arts in Copenhagen, and his wonderfully evocative
landscapes share space alongside
changing installations of mostly
Icelandic 20th-century paintings.
(☑411 6420; www.artmuseum.is; Flókagata

24, Miklatún Park; adult/child kr1300/free;
⏱10am-5pm)

Ásgrímur Jónsson Collection

ART MUSEUM

6 ⊙ Map p54, A4

Iceland's first professional painter,
Ásgrímur Jónsson (1876–1958) was the
son of a farmer. He lived and worked
here, and you can visit his former atel-
ier to see his work incorporating folk
tales and Icelandic nature. (☎515 9625;
www.listasafn.is; Bergstaðastræti 74; adult/
child kr1000/free; ⏱2-5pm Tue, Thu & Sun
mid-May–mid-Sep, 2-5pm Sun mid-Sep–Nov &
Feb–mid-May)

Einar Jónsson Museum

ART MUSEUM

7 ⊙ Map p54, C4

Einar Jónsson (1874–1954) is one of
Iceland's foremost sculptors, famous
for intense symbolist works. Chis-
elled representations of Hope, Earth
and Death burst from basalt cliffs,
weep over naked women and slay
dragons. Jónsson designed the building, which was built between 1916
and 1923, when this empty hill was
the outskirts of town. It also contains
his austere penthouse flat and
studio, with views over the city. The
sculpture garden (Freyjugata; admission
free; ⏱24hr) behind the museum
contains 26 bronzes, in the shadow
of Hallgrímskirkja. (☎551 3797; www.
lej.is; Eiriksgata 3; adult/child kr1000/free;
⏱10am-5pm Tue-Sun)

Top Tip

Donating to the Icelandic Phallological Museum

The acquisition of Páll Arason's
'specimen' by the Icelandic Phallological Museum was the subject
of oddball documentary *The Final
Member* (2012). Five other donors-
in-waiting have already promised
to bequeath their manhood (signed
contracts are mounted on the wall).
Interested? Get in line.

Sundhöllin

GEOTHERMAL POOL, HOT-POT

8 ⊙ Map p54, D4

Reykjavík's oldest swimming pool
(1937), designed in art-deco style
by architect Guðjón Samúelsson, is
smack in the city centre and offers
the only indoor pool within the city,
plus Hallgrímskirkja views from the
decks. It's been recently renovated.
(☎411 5350; Barónsstígur 16; adult/child
kr900/140; ⏱6.30am-10pm Mon-Thu, to
8pm Fri, 8am-4pm Sat, 10am-6pm Sun; 👶)

Sun Voyager

SCULPTURE

9 ⊙ Map p54, D2

Reykjavík is adorned with fascinating
sculptures, but it's Jón Gunnar Árnason's shiplike *Sun Voyager (Sólfar)*
sculpture that seems to catch visitors'
imaginations. Scooping in a skeletal
arc along the seaside, it offers a photo
shoot with snowcapped mountains in
the distance. (Sólfar; Sæbraut)

Local Life

Design, Art & Craft

Get involved with graphic design, cooking, arts, crafts, music...you name it! **Creative Iceland** (☑615 3500; www.creativeiceland.is) hooks you up with local creative people offering workshops in their art or craft. If you're a knitter, the half-day knitting workshops at **Icelandic Culture and Craft Workshops** (☑869 9913; www.cultureandcraft.com; courses from kr15,900) use Icelandic wool. **Iceland Design Centre** (Hönnunarmiðstöð; ☑771 2200; www.icelanddesign.is; Aðalstræti 2; ⊙10am-6pm Mon-Sat) lists more artists, designers and special events.

Árnarhóll   LANDMARK

| 10 ◉ | Map p54, B2 |

A statue of Iceland's first settler, Ingólfur Arnarson, takes pride of place at Árnarhóll, a greensward that is also a central gathering place for parades and demonstrations.

Eating

Dill   ICELANDIC $$$

| 11 ✖ | Map p54, B2 |

Top 'New Nordic' cuisine is the major drawcard at this elegant yet simple bistro. The focus is very much on the food – locally sourced produce served as a parade of courses. The owners are friends with Copenhagen's famous Noma clan, and take Icelandic cuisine to similarly heady heights. Popular with locals and visitors alike, a reservation is a must. (☑552 1522; www.dillrestaurant.is; Hverfisgata 12; 5-course meal from kr11,900; ⊙6-10pm Wed-Sat)

Snaps   FRENCH $$

| 12 ✖ | Map p54, B3 |

Reserve ahead for this French bistro that's a mega-hit with locals. Snaps' secret is simple: serve scrumptious seafood and classic bistro mains (think steak or *moules frites*) at surprisingly decent prices. Lunch specials (11.30am to 2pm; kr1990) and scrummy brunches (11.30am to 4pm Saturday and Sunday; kr1300 to kr4000) are a big draw, too. (☑511 6677; www2.snaps.is; Þórsgata 1; dinner mains kr3800-5000; ⊙7-10am daily, 11.30am-11pm Sun-Thu, to midnight Fri & Sat)

Gló   ORGANIC, VEGETARIAN $$

| 13 ✖ | Map p54, B3 |

Join the cool cats in this upstairs, airy restaurant serving fresh, large daily specials loaded with Asian-influenced herbs and spices. Though not exclusively vegetarian, it's a wonderland of raw and organic foods with your choice from a broad bar of elaborate salads, from root veggies to Greek. It also has branches in **Laugardalur** (Engjateigur 19; ⊙11am-9pm Mon-Fri) and **Kópavogur** (Hæðasmári 6; ⊙11am-9pm Mon-Fri, 11.30am-9pm Sat & Sun). (☑553 1111; www.glo.is; Laugavegur 20b; mains kr1200-

Icelandic Phallological Museum (p56)

2000; ⏰11am-10pm Mon-Fri, 11.30am-10pm Sat & Sun; 🛜🖊️)

Þrír Frakkar
ICELANDIC, SEAFOOD **$$$**

14 Map p54, B4

Owner-chef Úlfar Eysteinsson has built up a consistently excellent reputation at this snug little restaurant – apparently a favourite of Jamie Oliver's. Specialities range throughout the aquatic world from salt cod and halibut to *plokkfiskur* (fish stew) with black bread. Non-fish items run towards guillemot, horse and lamb. (☑552 3939; www.3frakkar. com; Baldursgata 14; mains kr4000-6000; ⏰11.30am-2.30pm & 6-10pm Mon-Fri, 6-11pm Sat & Sun)

Ostabúðin
DELI **$$**

15 Map p54, B2

Head to this gourmet cheese shop and deli, with a large dining room for the friendly owner's cheese

Local Life
Brunch with Björk

Blink and you'll miss **Grái Kötturinn** (Map p54, B2; ☑551 1544; Hverfisgata 16a; mains kr1000-2300; ⏰7.15am-2pm Mon-Fri, 8am-2pm Sat & Sun), a tiny six-table cafe and favourite of Björk. It looks like a cross between an eccentric bookshop and an art gallery, and serves toast, bagels, pancakes, or bacon and eggs served on freshly baked bread.

and meat platters (from kr1900 to kr4000), or the catch of the day, accompanied by homemade bread. You can pick up other local goods, like terrines and duck confit, on the way out. (Cheese Shop; 📞 562 2772; www.facebook.com/Ostabudin/; Skólavörðustígur 8; mains kr3600-5000; ⏲restaurant 11.30am-9pm Mon-Fri, noon-9pm Sat & Sun, deli 10am-6pm Mon-Thu, to 7pm Fri, 11am-4pm Sat)

Restó
SEAFOOD $$

16 Map p54, E4

This homey little restaurant is over by Hlemmur Sq but it's worth the trek for delicious changing menus

---

Local Life
The Great Icelandic Bake-Off

Get out there and weigh in on the contest for Reykjavík's best bakery. **Bakarí Sandholt** (Map p54, C3; 📞 551 3524; www.sandholt.is; Laugavegur 36; snacks kr600-1200; ⏲7am-9pm; 📶) is usually crammed with folks hoovering up the generous assortment of fresh baguettes, croissants, pastries and sandwiches. The soup of the day comes with delicious sourdough bread. Or queue for some of the city's best home-baked breads and pastries at tiny new **Brauð & Co** (Map p54, C3; www.braudogco.is; Frakkastígur 16; ⏲6am-6pm Mon-Fri, to 5pm Sat & Sun), where you can watch Viking hipsters make the goodies while you wait.

---

of seafood, and the friendly family who runs the place. The owner-chef Jóhann Helgi Jóhannesson was the chef at celebrated seafood joint Ostabúðin, and he and his wife, Ragnheiður Helena Eðvarðsdóttir, have created a new anchor in this up-and-coming district. (📞 546 9550; www.resto.is; Rauðarárstígur 27-29; mains kr3600-5000; ⏲5.30-10pm Sun-Thu, to 10.30pm Fri & Sat)

Vegamót
INTERNATIONAL $$

17 Map p54, B3

A long-running bistro-bar-club, with a name that means 'crossroads', this is a perennially popular place to eat, drink, see and be seen at night (it's favoured by families during the day). The 'global' menu ranges all over: from Mexican salad to Louisiana chicken. Weekend brunches (kr1500 to kr3000) are a hit, too. (📞 511 3040; www.vegamot.is; Vegamótastígur 4; lunch mains kr1500-2900, dinner mains kr1500-4500; ⏲11am-10pm Sun-Wed, to 11pm Thu, to 11.30pm Fri & Sat, bar to 1am Sun-Thu, to 4am Fri & Sat; 📶)

Public House
FUSION, TAPAS $$

18 Map p54, C3

Excellent Asian-style tapas and great local draught beers and cocktails are only part of the draw to this new central gastropub. It's also just a fun place to hang out, with its bustling dining room and tables spilling out onto Laugavegur. A place to see and be seen. (📞555 7333; www.publichouse.is; Laugavegur 24; small plates kr1300-2000; 🕑11.30am-1am)

Sushisamba   FUSION $$$

19 Map p54, B2

Sushisamba is a perennial capital favourite for sushi, and puts an international spin on straight-up sushi, alongside meat and seafood mains. (📞568 6600; www.sushisamba.is; Þingholtsstræti 5; sushi kr1300-4000, multicourse menus kr8000-9000; 🕑5-11pm Sun-Thu, to midnight Fri & Sat)

Kolabrautin   ITALIAN $$$

20 Map p54, B1

Kolabrautin, high up on the top of the Harpa concert hall, creatively uses Icelandic ingredients with Mediterranean techniques. Start with a splashy cocktail before digging into dishes like cod with lobster cream. (📞519 9700; www.kolabrautin.is; Harpa concert hall, Austurbakki 2; mains kr5500; 🕑5.30-11pm)

Garðurinn   VEGETARIAN $

21 Map p54, B3

This small, friendly restaurant serves up ever-changing vegetarian and vegan soups and dishes of the day. (www.kaffigardurinn.is; Klapparstígur 37; mains kr1300-2000; 🕑11am-6.30pm Mon, Tue, Thu & Fri, to 5pm Wed, noon-5pm Sat; ✒)

Joylato   ICE CREAM $

22 Map p54, B3

Scoops of high-end homemade ice cream and sorbets in delectable flavours. Some are made from cashew or coconut milk. (www.joylato.is; Njálsgata 1; scoops kr850; 🕑3-10pm Thu-Tue, to 5.30pm Wed)

The Cafe Scene

The city's ratio of coffeehouses to citizens is staggering. The folks at **Reykjavík Roasters** (Map p54, C3; www.reykjavikroasters.is; Kárastígur 1; ☺8am-6pm Mon-Fri, 9am-5pm Sat & Sun) take their coffee seriously, and it's the first stop for local coffee aficionados. It has a sunny new **branch** (Brautarholt 2; ☺8am-6pm Mon-Fri, 9am-5pm Sat & Sun; 🛜) in the Hlemmur area. Or soak up the vibe at Reykjavík's oldest coffee shop, **Kaffi Mokka** (Map p54, B3; 📞552 1174; www.mokka.is; Skólavörðustígur 3a; ☺9am-6.30pm), where little has changed since the 1950s, from its original mosaic pillars and copper lights to its waffles, sandwiches and coffees.

Drinking

Kaffi Vínyl   CAFE

23 📍 Map p54, D3

This new entry on the Reykjavík coffee, restaurant and music scene is popular for its chill vibe, great music, and delicious vegan and vegetarian food. (📞537 1332; www.facebook.com/vinilrvk/; Hverfisgata 76; ☺9am-11pm Mon-Fri, 10am-11pm Sat, noon-11pm Sun; 🛜)

Loft Hostel Bar   BAR

24 📍 Map p54, B2

This lively patio bar, at the hostel of the same name, draws visitors and locals alike, especially for its happy

hour from 4pm to 7pm. (www.lofthostel.is; Bankastræti 7)

Bravó   BAR

25 📍 Map p54, B3

Friendly, knowledgeable bartenders, a laid-back corner-bar vibe with great people-watching, cool tunes on the sound system and happy-hour (11am to 8pm) draught local beers for kr650 – what's not to love? (Laugavegur 22; ☺11am-1am Mon-Thu, to 3am Fri & Sat; 🛜)

KEX Bar   BAR

26 📍 Map p54, D3

Locals like this hostel bar-restaurant (mains kr1800 to kr2600) in an old cookie factory (*kex* means cookie) for its broad windows facing the sea, courtyard and kids' play area. Happy hipsters soak up the 1920s Vegas vibe: saloon doors, old-school barber station, scuffed floors and chatter. (www.kexhostel.is; Skúlagata 28; ☺11.30am-11pm; 🛜)

Petersen Svítan   LOUNGE

27 📍 Map p54, B2

Get wide open views from this lounge bar on the roof of a restored old theatre (which occasionally hosts events). (Gamla Bíó; 📞563 4000; http://gamlabio.tji.li; Ingólfsstræti 2a; ☺11.30am-1am Sun-Thu, to 3am Fri & Sat)

Den Danske Kro   BAR

28 📍 Map p54, B2

This popular new bar is 'the Danish bar', and offers good cocktails and a

Iceland Design Centre (p58)

buzzy front deck. (Danski Barinn; www.danski.is; Ingólfsstræti 3; ☾noon-1am Sun-Thu, to 4.30am Fri & Sat)

Bar Ananas
BAR

29 Map p54, B3

This tropical-themed bar is a good bet for warming up for a night out. (Klapparstígur 38; ☾5pm-1am Sun-Thu, to 3am Fri & Sat)

C is for Cookie
CAFE

30 Map p54, B3

Named in honour of Sesame Street's Cookie Monster, this cheerful spot has super coffee, plus great home-made cakes, salad, soup and grilled sandwiches. (Týsgata 8; ☾7.30am-6pm Mon-Fri, 11am-5pm Sat, noon-5pm Sun)

Kaffifélagið
CAFE

31 Map p54, B2

A popular hole-in-the-wall for a quick cuppa on the run, with a couple of outdoor tables, too. (www.kaffifelagid.is; Skólavörðustígur 10; ☾7.30am-6pm Mon-Fri, 10am-4pm Sat)

Kigali Kaffi
CAFE

32 Map p54, B2

Excellent Rwandan fair-trade coffee in a small new coffeeshop. (www.facebook.com/kigali.kaffi; Ingólfsstræti 8; ☾10am-6pm Mon-Fri, 11am-8pm Sat)

Entertainment

Bíó Paradís   CINEMA

33 ⭐ Map p54, C3

This totally cool cinema, decked out in movie posters and vintage officeware, screens specially curated Icelandic films with English subtitles. It's a chance to see movies that you may not find elsewhere. Plus there's a happy hour from 5pm to 7.30pm. (www.bio paradis.is; Hverfisgata 54; adult kr1600; 🛜)

Local Life
Icelandic Music

The den of musical goodness that is **Lucky Records** (Map p54, E4; 📞 551 1195; www.luckyrecords.is; Rauðarárstígur 10; ⏰10am-6pm Mon-Fri, 11am-5pm Sat & Sun) holds loads of modern Icelandic music, but plenty of vintage vinyl too. The huge collection spans from hip hop to electronica, and there's occasional live music. **12 Tónar** (Map p54, B3; www.12tonar.is; Skolavörðustígur 15; ⏰10am-6pm Mon-Sat, from noon Sun) has launched some of Iceland's favourite bands. The two-floor shop is a very cool place to hang out: listen to CDs, drink coffee and sometimes catch a live performance. Or, scratch your vinyl itch at **Reykjavík Record Shop** (Map p54, B2; 📞561 2299; www.facebook. com/reykjavikrecordshop; Klapparstígur 35; ⏰11am-6pm Mon-Fri, to 5pm Sat, 1-5pm Sun), in the city centre.

Mengi   LIVE PERFORMANCE

34 ⭐ Map p54, B3

This new entry on the gallery and performance art scene may be small, but it offers an innovative program of music and performing arts. (📞588 3644; www.mengi.net; Óðinsgata 2; ⏰noon-6pm Tue-Sat & for performances)

Café Rosenberg   LIVE MUSIC

35 ⭐ Map p54, C2

This big, booklined shopfront is dotted with couches and cocktail tables, and hosts all manner of live acts, from local singer-songwriters to jazz groups, with broad-paned windows looking onto the street. (📞551 2442; Klapparstígur 25-27; ⏰3pm-1am Mon-Thu, 4pm-3am Fri & Sat)

National Theatre   THEATRE

36 ⭐ Map p54, B2

The National Theatre has three separate stages and puts on plays, musicals and operas, from modern Icelandic works to Shakespeare. (Þjóðleikhúsið; 📞551 1200; www.leikhusid.is; Hverfisgata 19; ⏰closed Jul)

Shopping

Kraum   ARTS & CRAFTS

The brainchild of a band of local artists, Kraum literally means 'simmering', like the island's quaking earth and the inventive minds of its citizens. Expect a fascinating assortment of unique designer wares, like fish-skin apparel and driftwood furniture. Find it downstairs in the large Cintamani store (see 24 🅟 Map p54, B2). (www.kraum.is; Bankastræti 7; ⏱9am-7pm Mon-Fri, 10am-6pm Sat, 11am-6pm Sun)

Skúmaskot ARTS & CRAFTS

37 🅐 Map p54, B3

Ten local designers create these unique handmade porcelain items, women's and kids' clothing, paintings and cards. It's in a recently renovated large gallery beautifully showcasing their creative Icelandic crafts. (🕿663 1013; www.facebook.com/skumaskot.art.design/; Skólavörðustígur 21a; ⏱10am-6pm Mon-Fri, to 5pm Sat, noon-4pm Sun)

Kiosk CLOTHING

38 🅐 Map p54, D3

This wonderful designers' cooperative is lined with creative women's fashion in a glass-fronted boutique. Designers take turns (wo)manning the store. (🕿445 3269; www.kioskreykjavik.com; Laugavegur 65; ⏱11am-6pm Mon-Fri, to 5pm Sat)

Rammagerðin – Iceland Gift Store SOUVENIRS

39 🅐 Map p54, B3

One of the city's better souvenir shops, Rammagerðin offers loads of woollens, crafts and collectibles. It also has locations at Skólavörðustígur 12, Bankastræti 9 and Keflavík

Top Tip

Shopping Icelandic Style

▶ Reykjavík's vibrant design culture makes for great shopping: from sleek, fish-skin purses and knitted *lopapeysur* (Icelandic woollen sweaters) to unique music or lip-smacking Icelandic schnapps *brennivín*.

▶ Laugavegur is the most dense shopping street. You'll find interesting shops all over town, but fashion concentrates near the Frakkastígur and Vitastígur end of Laugavegur.

▶ Skólavörðustígur is strong for arts and jewellery. Bankastræti and Austurstræti have many touristy shops.

▶ Don't forget – all visitors are eligible for a 15% tax refund on their shopping, under certain conditions.

International Airport. (🕿535 6690; www.icelandgiftstore.com; Skólavörðustígur 12; ⏱9am-10pm)

Orrifinn JEWELLERY

40 🅐 Map p54, B3

Subtle, beautiful jewellery captures the natural wonder of Iceland and its Viking history. Delicate anchors, axes and pen nibs dangle from understated matte chains. (🕿789 7616; www.facebook.com/OrrifinnJewels/; Skólavörðustíg 17a; ⏱10am-6pm Mon-Fri, to 4pm Sat)

Beautiful Stories
CLOTHING

41 🔒 Map p54, C3

Dreamy, feminine designs beg for browsing. Hip lace, silk and swingy little dresses are the order of the day. (www.beautifulstoriesclothes.com; Laugavegur 46; ⏰10am-6pm Mon-Fri, to 5pm Sat, 1-5pm Sun)

Local Life
Knitting & Woolly Wear

If you've got a hankering for some of the local knitwear, **Handknitting Association of Iceland** (Handprjónasamband Íslands; Map p54, B3; 📞552 1890; www.hand knit.is; Skólavörðustígur 19; ⏰9am-10pm Mon-Fri, to 6pm Sat, 10am-6pm Sun) sells traditional handmade hats, socks and sweaters, or you can buy yarn, needles and knitting patterns and do it yourself. The association's smaller **branch** (Map p54, C3; 📞562 1890; Laugavegur 53b; ⏰9am-7pm Mon-Fri, 10am-5pm Sat) sells made-up items only. **Álafoss** (Map p54, B2; 📞562 6303; www. alafoss.is; Laugavegur 8; ⏰10am-6pm) stocks hand- or machine-made *lopapeysur* (Icelandic woollen sweaters) and other wool products. Its **outlet store** (📞566 6303; www.alafoss.is; Álafossvegur 23, Mosfellsbær; ⏰9am-6pm Mon-Fri, to 4pm Sat; 🚌15) in Mosfellsbær also sells yarn and needles.

Mál og Menning
BOOKS

42 🔒 Map p54, B3

Friendly, popular and well-stocked independent bookshop carries great English-language books for getting under the skin of Iceland. Check out *Thermal Pools in Iceland* by Jón G Snæland and Þóra Sigurbjörnsdóttir; you can browse it in the lively cafe. Also sells CDs, games and newspapers. (📞580 5000; www.bmm.is; Laugavegur 18; ⏰9am-10pm Mon-Fri, 10am-10pm Sat; 🛜)

KronKron
CLOTHING

43 🔒 Map p54, D3

This is where Reykjavík goes high fashion, with the likes of Marc Jacobs and Vivienne Westwood. But we really enjoy its Scandinavian designers (including Kron by KronKron) offering silk dresses, knit capes, scarves and even wool underwear. Its handmade shoes are off the charts – also sold down the street at **Kron** (📞551 8388; www.kron. is; Laugavegur 48; ⏰10am-6pm Mon-Thu, to 6.30pm Fri, to 5pm Sat). (📞562 8388; www. kronkron.com; Laugavegur 63b; ⏰10am-6pm Mon-Thu, to 6.30pm Fri, to 5pm Sat)

Geysir
CLOTHING

44 🔒 Map p54, B3

If you're looking for traditional Icelandic clothing and unique modern designs, Geysir boasts an elegant selection of sweaters, blankets, and men's and women's clothes, shoes and bags. There's also a branch down the street at Skólavörðustígur 7. (📞519

6000; www.geysir.com; Skólavörðustígur 16;
⏱9am-10pm)

Jör   CLOTHING

45 🔒 Map p54, D3

Chic clothing is the order of the day at
the trendy boutique of Guðmundur Jörundsson, who designs everything from
strappy lingerie to sleek menswear.
(📞546 1303; www.jorstore.com; Laugavegur
89; ⏱10am-6pm Mon-Sat, 1-5pm Sun)

Blue Lagoon Shop   COSMETICS

46 🔒 Map p54, B2

Forgot to stock up on facial masks and
unguents at the Blue Lagoon? Here's
your chance! You'll also find its line of
beauty products at Lyfa pharmacies,
Hagkaup and Keflavík International
Airport duty free. (📞420 8849; www.
bluelagoon.com; Laugavegur 15; ⏱10am-6pm
Mon-Fri, to 4pm Sat, 1-5pm Sun)

Reykjavík's Cutest   ARTS & CRAFTS

47 🔒 Map p54, C3

Follow the painted path to the polka-
dotted house just back from Laugavegur for a great selection of handmade
souvenirs and crafts. (Laugavegur 27;
⏱10am-8pm May-Sep, to 6pm Oct-Apr)

Hrím   DESIGN

48 🔒 Map p54, C3

With one large high-concept design
store, and one smaller kitchenware
store (Laugavegur 32), Hrím stands

⬤ Local Life
Outdoors Outfitters

Iceland's premier outdoor-clothing
companies **66° North** (Map p54, B2;
📞535 6680; www.66north.is; Bankastræti
5; ⏱9am-10pm) began by making all-
weather wear for Arctic fishermen.
This metamorphosed into costly,
fashionable streetwear; jackets,
fleeces, hats and gloves, like those
of **Cintamani** (Map p54, B2; 📞533
3390; www.cintamani.is; Bankastræti 7;
⏱9am-10pm). If you're looking to
outfit for hiking or camping, your
best bet is **Gangleri Outfitters** (Map
p54, D3; 📞583 2222; www.outfitters.
is; Hverfisgata 82; ⏱10am-7pm Mon-Fri,
11am-5pm Sat & Sun), with gear sales
and rentals: tents, sleeping bags,
stoves, backpacks, boots, GPS etc.
Fjallakofinn (Map p54, B2; 📞510 9505;
www.fjallakofinn.is; Laugavegur 11; ⏱9am-
7pm Mon-Fri, 10am-5pm Sat, noon-6pm
Sun) offers (pricey) brand-name
camping and climbing gear, GoPros
and more, plus equipment rental,
as does **Iceland Camping Equipment Rental** (Map p54, D3 📞647 0569;
www.iceland-camping-equipment.com;
Barónsstígur 5; ⏱9am-5pm May-Oct, by
appointment Nov-Apr).

out for its creative Scandinavian and
high-end tchotchkes, linens and other
eminently take-home-able gear. (www.
hrim.is; Laugavegur 25; ⏱10am-8pm Mon-
Thu, to 6.30pm Fri, to 6pm Sat, 1-6pm Sun)

Local Life
Laugardalur

The verdant park at Laugardalur, 4km east of the centre, was once the main source of Reykjavík's hot water: Laugardalur means 'Hot Springs Valley', and you'll still find relics from the old wash house. Laugardalur is a favourite of locals for its huge geo-thermal swimming complex, spa, arenas, skating rink, botanical gardens, cafe and kids' zoo and entertainment park. Nearby are top museums and a farmers market.

Getting There

🚌 **Bus** 2, 5, 14, 15 or 17 pass 200m from Laugardalur park; 14 is closest to the pool.

🚌 **Bus** Route 16 serves the waterfront and Sigurjón Ólafsson Museum.

Skafarbakki Harbour, Viðey Island ferry (200m)

Sæbraut

Laugalækur

Hrísateigur

Sundlaugavegur

Reykjavegur

Camping

LAUGARDALUR

Laugarásvegur

Laugardalsvöllur National Stadium

Old Wash House

Sigtún

Laugardalshöllin

Reykjavík Skating Hall

Café Flóra

Ármúli

Engjavegur

Vegmúli

Suðurlandsbraut

Laugardalur

0 ——— 400 m
0 ——— 0.2 miles

❶ Local Art

Visit Ásmundur Sveinsson's playful sculptures at Reykjavík Art Museum's **Ásmundarsafn** (Ásmundur Sveinsson Museum; ☎ 411 6430; www.artmuseum.is; Sigtún; adult/child kr1500/free; ⏰ 10am-5pm May-Sep, 1-5pm Oct-Apr; 🚌 2, 5, 15, 17). Monumental concrete creations fill the garden, while inside are works in wood, clay and metals. Visit the dome: acoustics create the museum's 'must-sing policy'.

❷ Hot Springs

Reykjavík's naturally hot water is the heart of the city's social life. **Laugardalslaug** (☎ 411 5100; Sundlaugavegur 30a, Laugardalur; adult/child kr900/140, suit/towel rental kr850/570; ⏰ 6.30am-10pm Mon-Fri, 8am-10pm Sat & Sun; ♿) has the largest, best facilities: Olympic-sized pools, seven hot-pots, saltwater tub, steam bath and curling 86m water slide.

❸ Workout & Pampering

Super-duper **Laugar Spa** (☎ 553 0000; www.laugarspa.com; Sundlaugavegur 30a, Laugardalur; day pass kr5490; ⏰ 6am-11.30pm Mon-Fri, 8am-10pm Sat, to 8pm Sun) offers six saunas and steam rooms; a seawater tub; a vast, well-equipped gym; a cafe; fitness classes; and beauty and massage clinics. The spa is 18+ and includes access to Laugardalslaug.

❹ Gourmet Gardens

The **Reykjavík Botanic Gardens** (Grasagarður; ☎ 411 8650; www.grasagardur. is; Laugardalur; admission free; ⏰ 10am-10pm May-Sep, to 3pm Oct-Apr; 🚌 2, 5, 14, 15, 17) contain over 5000 varieties of subarctic plant species, colourful seasonal flowers and birdlife, and a wonderful summer cafe, **Café Flóra** (Flóran; ☎ 553 8872; www.floran.is; Botanic Gardens; cakes kr950, mains kr1400-3000; ⏰ 10am-10pm May-Sep; ♿).

❺ Family Fun

The **Reykjavík Zoo & Family Park** (Fjölskyldu og Húsdýragarðurinn; ☎ 411 5900; www.mu.is; Laugardalur; adult/child kr840/620, 1-/10-/20-ride ticket kr310/2500/4650, multi-ride pass kr2150; ⏰ 10am-6pm Jun–mid-Aug, to 5pm mid-Aug–May; 👶; 🚌 2, 5, 15, 17) gets packed with happy local families. Don't expect lions; think seals, foxes and farm animals. The family park section has a mini-racetrack, child-size bulldozers, a giant trampoline, boats and rides.

❻ Shop Local

Frú Lauga (☎ 534 7165; www.frulauga.is; Laugalækur 6; ⏰ 11am-6pm Mon-Fri, to 4pm Sat; ♿) farmers market sources its products from all over the countryside. Sample *skyr* desserts from Erpsstaðir farm, organic vegetables, meats, curated international chocolates, wine and the like.

❼ Waterfront Sculpture & Walks

The peaceful seafront studio of sculptor Sigurjón Ólafsson (1908–82) is now the **Sigurjón Ólafsson Museum** (Listasafn Sigurjóns Ólafssonar; ☎ 553 2906; www.lso.is; Laugarnestanga 70; adult/child kr1000/free; ⏰ 2-5pm Tue-Sun Jun-Aug, 2-5pm Sat & Sun Sep-Nov & Feb-May; 🚌 12, 16), showcasing his powerful busts and driftwood totem poles.

Local Life
Viðey Island

Getting There

⚓ **Ferry** Depart from Skarfabakki year-round (weekends-only in winter) and Harpa and the Old Harbour in summer.

🚌 **Bus** 16 stops near Skarfabakki; on the tour-bus route.

On fine-weather days, the tiny uninhabited island of Viðey (www.reykjavikmuseum.is) makes a wonderful day trip. You can enjoy occasional cultural tours with varying themes in summer, while in late August, some Reykjavikers come to pick wild caraway. Less than 1km off Reykjavík's Skarfabakki harbour, it feels a world away. Surprising modern artworks, an abandoned village and great bird-watching add to its remote spell. The only sounds are the wind, the waves and golden bumblebees buzzing among the tufted vetch and hawkweed.

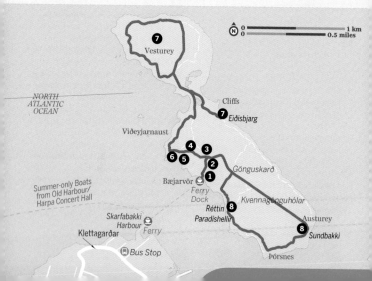

❶ Viðeyarstofa & Church

Skúli Magnússon (1711–94), the power-ful sheriff, built Viðeyarstofa as his home here in the 1750s. Now it houses a **cafe** (mains kr2300-3700; ⏱11.30am-5pm mid-May–Sep, 1.30-4pm Sat & Sun Oct–mid-May; 🛜) serving basic fare like burgers and waffles. Explore the adjacent 18th-century wooden church with Skúli's tomb.

❷ Local History

Viðey was settled around AD900 and farmed until the 1950s. It was home to a powerful monastery from 1225, but in 1539 it was wiped out by Dan-ish soldiers during the Reformation. Look for the remains of the monastery behind the Viðeyarstofa.

❸ Explore the Island

The whole island is criss-crossed with walking paths. Some you can bicycle, others are more precarious. A good map at the harbour shows which are which. The island is great for bird-watching (30 species breed here) and botany (over one-third of all Icelandic plants grow on the island).

❹ Bike It

In summer you can hire a bike at the Old Harbour at **Reykjavík Bike Tours** (Reykjavík Segway Tours; 📱 bike 694 8956, segway 897 2790; www.icelandbike.com; Ægisgarður 7, Old Harbour; bike rental per 4hr from kr3500, tours from kr6500; ⏱9am-5pm Jun-Aug, reduced hours Sep-May; 🚌14) and

bring it with you on the ferry. There's nothing quite like the free, wind-in-your-hair feeling of cycling along the island paths.

❺ Wander the Art

Visit Yoko Ono's **Imagine Peace Tower** (2007), a 'wishing well' that blasts a dazzling column of light into the sky every night between 9 October (John Lennon's birthday) and 8 December (the anniversary of his death). See Viðey's website for Peace Tower tours from Reykjavík.

❻ Barbecue

Locals in the know come prepared with cook-out supplies and head to glass-fronted Viðeyjarnaust day-hut, on a beautiful headland, which has a public barbecue.

❼ To the North

Trails leading northwest take you around ponds, some monuments to shipwrecks, the low cliffs of Eiðisb-jarg, and Vesturey at the northern tip of the island. Richard Serra's huge basalt sculptures, **Áfangar** (Standing Stones; 1990), dot this part of the island.

❽ Southern Ruins

Trails to the southeast lead past the natural sheepfold **Réttin**, the tiny grotto **Paradíshellir** (Paradise Cave), and then to the abandoned fishing village at **Sundbakki**.

Top Experiences
Blue Lagoon

Getting There

🚌 **Bus** Reykjavík Excursions (www.re.is) connects Reykjavík, the airport and the lagoon.

💟 **Tours** Many come here; check if you need to book your lagoon ticket separately.

In a magnificent black-lava field, 47km southwest of Reykjavík, this milky-teal spa is fed by water (at a perfect 38°C) from futuristic Svartsengi geothermal plant. Those who say it's too commercial aren't wrong, but the colour and feel of the water is truly other-worldly, and with the roiling steam clouds and people daubed in white mud, you'll feel like you're on another planet.

A Good Soak

The super-heated spa water (70% sea water, 30% fresh water) is rich in blue-green algae, mineral salts and fine silica mud, which condition and exfoliate the skin – sounds like advertising speak, but you really do come out as soft as a baby's bum.

Explore the Complex

The lagoon has an enormous complex of changing rooms, restaurants, a rooftop viewpoint and a gift shop. At the pool you'll find hot-pots, steam rooms, a sauna, a floating noodle station, a silica-mask station, a bar and a piping-hot waterfall that delivers a powerful hydraulic massage – like being pummelled by a troll. A VIP section has its own wading space, lounge and viewing platform.

Massage

For extra relaxation, lie on a floating mattress and have a massage therapist knead your knots (30/60 minutes €75/120). Book spa treatments well in advance; look online for packages and winter rates.

Stay Longer

If you thrive on remote lava fields and extensive spa time, **Blue Lagoon – Silica Hotel** (📞420 8806; www.bluelagoon.com; d incl breakfast kr51,600; P @ 🛜 🏊) and **Northern Light Inn** (📞426 8650; www.northernlightinn.is; s/d incl breakfast kr28,500/37,500; P @ 🛜) are both walking distance from the lagoon. A five-star hotel is being built on the property, too, and was expected to open in 2017.

Nearby: Cycle & Quad

Combine your Blue Lagoon visit with myriad package tours, or hook up with nearby ATV Adventures (p75) for cycling or quad-bike tours or bicycle rental. It picks up and drops off at the lagoon.

Bláa Lónið

📞 420 8800

www.bluelagoon.com

adult/child Jun-Aug from €50/free, Sep-May from €40/free

🕐 8am-midnight Jun–mid-Aug, reduced hours low season

☑ Top Tips

▶ There is an hourly cap on admissions; book ahead. The lagoon can sell out days in advance.

▶ Get e-ticket deals from the website or tour company vouchers (Iceland Air, Reykjavík Excursions).

▶ Avoid summertime between 10am and 2pm – go early or after 7pm.

✕ Take a Break

Blue Café (snacks kr1000-2100; 🕐 8am-midnight Jun–mid-Aug, reduced hours mid-Aug–May; 🛜) has cafeteria-style eats, while **LAVA Restaurant** (📞420 8800; www.bluelagoon.com; mains lunch/dinner kr4500/5900; 🕐 11.30am-9.30pm Jun-Aug, to 8.30pm Sep-May; 🛜) features Icelandic dishes.

Q Local Life
Reykjanes Peninsula

Getting There

🚗 **Car** Best way to travel.

🚌 **Bus** From Keflavík town, Strætó (www.bus.is) bus 89 serves Garður and Sandgerði, bus 55 goes to Reykjavík and 88 connects to Grindavík.

The Reykjanes Peninsula (www.visitreykjanes.is) is special not only for the Blue Lagoon, Iceland's most famous attraction, but for other local favourites. Sweet fishing hamlets Garður and Sandgerði sit minutes to the west of the airport. Untamed landscapes of volcanic craters, mineral lakes, hot springs and rugged, ATV-ready mountains and coastal lava fields stretch from Reykjanestá to the Reykjanesfólkvangur Wilderness Reserve.

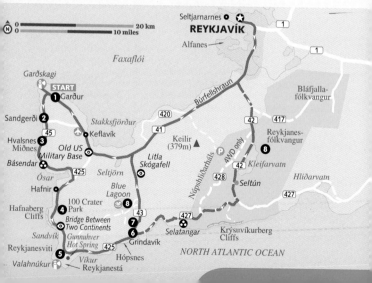

1 Garður

Garður's beautiful windswept **Garðskagi headland** is great for birdwatching and sometimes seal or whale spotting. Two quaint lighthouses add drama. There's a small folk museum, too.

2 Local History & Seafood

In Sandgerði, peruse the fascinating exhibit about shipwrecked explorer Jean-Baptiste Charcot at the **Sudurnes Science and Learning Center** (📞423 7551; www.thekkingarsetur.is; Gerðavegur 1; adult/child kr600/300; ⏰10am-4pm Mon-Fri, 1-5pm Sat & Sun May-Sep, 10am-2pm Mon-Fri Oct-Apr). Enjoy a seafood lunch at excellent **Vitinn** (📞423 7755; www.vitinn.is; Vitatorg 7; mains kr2000-4300; ⏰11.30am-2pm & 6-9pm Mon-Sat).

3 Birds & Bards

Pleasant **beaches** dot the coast south of Sandgerði, and the surrounding marshes are frequented by more than 190 species of **birds**. You'll find a lonely church at **Hvalsnes**, featured in a famous Icelandic hymn by Hallgrímur Pétursson (1616–74), written at the death of his young daughter who was buried here.

4 100 Crater Park

In the far southwest of the peninsula, the lava fields and wild volcanic craters are dubbed 100 Crater Park. Power plants exploit geothermal heat to produce salt from seawater and to generate electricity. **Power Plant Earth** (Orkuverið Jörð; 📞436

1000; www.hsorka.is; Reykjanesvirkjun Power Plant; adult/child kr1500/1000; ⏰9am-4pm May-Aug) has an interactive exhibition about energy.

5 Valahnúkur

One of the most wild and wonderful spots on the peninsula is the lava fields at Valahnúkur. Dramatic, climbable **cliffs** and **Reykjanesviti lighthouse** sit near a multicoloured geothermal area with hot spring **Gunnuhver**.

6 Break in Grindavík

For a late-afternoon pick-me-up, stop off at charming dock-front cafe **Bryggjan** (📞426 7100; Miðgarður 2; cake kr850, soup kr1600-2000; ⏰8am-11pm; 📶), in Grindavík.

7 Open Air

To explore Reykjanes by foot, ATV or horse, Grindavík is home to outfitters **ATV Adventures** (📞857 3001; www.atv4x4.is) and **Arctic Horses** (📞848 0143; www.arctichorses.is; Hópsheiði 16), and the **tourist office** (📞420 1190; www.visitgrindavik.is; ⏰10am-5pm mid-May–mid-Sep) stocks maps of the region's walking trails.

8 Springs, Lava & Lakes

Looping back to Reykjavík, visit either the **Blue Lagoon** (p72), late, like the locals, or the dramatic lava, hot springs and lakes around the 300-sq-km **Reykjanesfólkvangur Wilderness Reserve**.

Explore

Golden Circle

The Golden Circle takes in three popular attractions all within 100km of the capital: Þingvellir, Geysir and Gullfoss. It is an artificial tourist circuit (ie no natural topography marks its extent) loved by thousands. You'll see a meeting-point of the continental plates and site of the ancient Icelandic parliament (Þingvellir), a spouting hot spring (Geysir) and a roaring waterfall (Gullfoss), all in one doable-in-a-day loop.

The Region in a Day

☀️ Get an early start from Reykjavík and head straight to **Þingvellir** (p78), planning at least an hour to wander the parliament site, the rift and falls. On your way there you can visit the **Gljúfrasteinn Laxness Museum** (p88), the home of Nobel Prize–winning author Halldór Laxness.

☀️ Lunch on delicious wild-caught dishes in Laugarvatn at **Lindin** (p88), in its formal restaurant or laid-back bistro. Or head to **Efstidalur II** (p89) for local-caught fish and farm burgers; don't miss their farm ice cream and cool barn cafe. They also have horse riding. For a swank spa experience, take a dip at **Fontana** (p85). Then visit **Geysir** and **Strokkur** (p80; pictured left) and **Gullfoss** (p82). If time permits, squeeze in **river rafting** (p88) near Reykholt.

🌙 If you didn't hit the spa at Fontana be sure to spend your evening in Flúðir at **Gamla Laugin** (p85), a natural historic geothermal pool, newly and wonderfully refurbished, next to mini-geysers, meadows and a rushing brook. Afterwards, grab a bite at **Minilik** (p90), or stop in Selfoss at **Tryggvaskáli** (p89) or **Kaffi Krús** (p90) for Icelandic fare.

 Top Experiences

Þingvellir (p78)

Geysir (p80)

Gullfoss (p82)

💜 **Best of Golden Circle**

Eating
Lindin (p88)

For Free
Þingvellir (p78)

Geysir (p80)

Gullfoss (p82)

Getting There

🚗 **Car** Easiest way to tailor your trip.

🎯 **Tour** Myriad tours cover the Golden Circle.

🚌 **Bus** Key routes are with Reykjavík Excursions (p147), such as bus 6/6A (BSÍ Bus Station–Þingvellir–Laugarvatn–Geysir–Gullfoss, one daily mid-June to mid-September).

Top Experiences
Þingvellir

Unesco World Heritage Site Þingvellir National
Park (40km northeast of central Reykjavík) is
Iceland's most important historical spot. The
Viking settlers established the world's first demo-
cratic parliament, the Alþingi, here in AD 930.
Meetings were conducted outdoors in the superb
natural setting: an immense, fissured rift valley,
caused by the meeting of the North American
and Eurasian tectonic plates, with rivers and
waterfalls all around.

◉ Map p84, B1

www.thingvellir.is

Historic buildings, Þingvellir National Park

Tectonic Plates

Þingvellir sits on a tectonic plate boundary where North America and Europe are tearing away from each other at 1mm to 18mm per year. As a result, the plain is scarred by dramatic fissures and rivers, including the great rift **Almannagjá**. A path runs along the fault between the clifftop visitors centre and the Alþingi site. Look for the **Öxarárfoss** falls, on the northern edge of the cliffs.

Historic Buildings

The farmhouse in the bottom of the rift, **Þingvallabær**, was built for the 1000th anniversary of the Alþingi in 1930 by state architect Guðjón Samúelsson. It's now used as the park warden's office and prime minister's summer house. **Þingvallakirkja** (⊙9am-5pm Jun-Aug) was one of Iceland's first churches. The original was consecrated in the 11th century; the current building dates from 1859.

Encampment Ruins

Straddling the Öxará river are ruins of temporary camps called *búðir* (booths). These stone foundations were covered during sessions and also acted like stalls at today's music festivals: selling beer, food and vellum. Most date to the 17th and 18th centuries; the largest, and one of the oldest, is **Biskupabúð**, north of the church.

Alþingi

Near the dramatic Almannagjá fault and fronted by a boardwalk is the **Lögberg** (Law Rock), where the Alþingi convened annually, and where the *lögsögumaður* (law speaker) recited existing laws. After Iceland's conversion to Christianity the site shifted to the foot of the Almannagjá cliffs, which acted as a natural amplifier. That site is marked by the Icelandic flag.

☑ Top Tips

▶ **Þingvellir Information Centre** (Leirar Þjónustumiðstöð; ☎482 2660; www.thingvellir.is; ⊙9am-8pm May-Sep, to 5pm Oct-Apr), on Rte 36, on the north side of the lake, has details about the park, as does **Þingvellir Visitors Centre** (Gestastofa; ☎482 3613; ⊙9am-6:30pm Apr-Oct, to 5pm Nov-Mar) in the south.

▶ There are sometimes free guided tours in summer; check the website.

▶ There is a nominal parking fee, but no fee to enter the site.

✗ Take a Break

There's a **cafeteria** (soup kr990; ⊙9am-10pm Apr-Oct, reduced hours Nov-Mar) in the information centre on the north side of the lake, or the fab **Silfra Restaurant** (www.ioniceland.is; Nesjavellir vid Þingvallavatn; mains lunch kr2500-6000, dinner kr5000-7000; ⊙11.30am-10pm) at the Ion Luxury Adventure Hotel (on the south side of Þingvallavatn), which features slow-food ingredients.

Top Experiences
Geysir

One of Iceland's most famous tourist attractions, Geysir (*gay*-zeer; literally 'gusher') is the original hot-water spout after which all other geysers are named. Discovered in the beautiful Haukadalur geothermal region, the Great Geysir has been active for perhaps 800 years, and once gushed water up to 80m into the air. Now relatively dormant, its neighbour Strokkur steals the show with steady eruptions.

👁 Map p84, D1

admission free

Geysir & Strokkur

Geysir has gone through periods of lessened activity since around 1916. Earthquakes can stimulate activity, though nowadays eruptions are rare. Luckily for visitors, the reliable **Strokkur** sits alongside. You'll rarely wait more than 10 minutes for it to shoot an impressive 15m to 30m plume before vanishing down its enormous hole.

Geysir Center

The large Geysir Center corrals the masses across the street from the geysers. A souvenir shop of mall-like proportions with Icelandic name brands, and an N1 petrol station, share space with eateries.

Surrounding Activities

Enjoy Geysir's picturesque setting by hiking in nearby Haukadalur forest, hitting the links at **Geysir Golf Course** (Haukadalsvöllur; ☎ 893 8733; www.geysirgolf.is; 9 holes kr3000, club rental kr2500) or going salmon fishing on the Tungufljót river. On cold, clear winter evenings, look out for the Northern Lights. Many tours from Reykjavík offer these activities and more.

Adventure Tours

Iceland Safari (☎ 544 5454; www.icelandsafari.com), 1km south of Geysir, takes super-Jeep trips to places throughout the Southwest, or head 4km east of Geysir to Kjóastaðir horse farm where **Geysir Hestar** (☎ 847 1046; www.geysirhestar.com; Kjóastaðir 2) offers horse riding in the area or along Hvítá River Canyon to Gullfoss. **Rafting trips** (p88) ply the nearby Hvítá river.

DENNIS VAN DE WATER / SHUTTERSTOCK ©

☑ Top Tips

▶ Stand downwind only if you want a shower.

▶ The geothermal area containing Strokkur and Geysir was free to enter at the time of writing, though from time to time there is talk of instituting a fee.

▶ You can grab arresting photos from up the valley, looking back at the volcanic hills and erupting geyser.

✕ Take a Break

The **Geysir Center** (☎ 480 6800; www.geysircenter. com; ⏰ 10am-10pm Jun-Aug, to 6pm Sep-May; P 🛜 👶) houses a massive restaurant (mains kr2500 to kr5400), a cafe (mains kr1600 to kr3000) and a fast-food joint (mains kr990 to kr1990).

Across the street, the restaurant at **Hótel Geysir** (☎ 480 6800; www.geysircenter.is; Geysir Center; s/d incl breakfast kr18,000/22,900; P @ 🛜) bustles with tour groups tucking into lunch (threecourse meal kr7900).

Top Experiences
Gullfoss

Iceland's most famous waterfall, Gullfoss (Golden Falls) is a spectacular double cascade dropping a dramatic 32m. As it descends, it kicks up tiered walls of spray before thundering away down a narrow rocky ravine. On sunny days the mist creates shimmering rainbows, and it's also magical in winter when the falls glitter with ice. Though it's a popular sight, the falls' remote location still makes you feel the ineffable forces of nature that have been at work on this landscape for millennia.

Map p84, D1

www.gullfoss.is

admission free

Views & Photo Ops

A tarmac path leads from the main parking lot and visitor centre to a grand lookout over the falls. Stairs then continue down to the level of the falls. Alternatively, drive in on the spur below the tourist centre at falls-level for disabled-accessible parking. A path then continues down the valley toward the thundering falls for the most kinetic video shots.

Saving the Falls

Sigríður Tómasdóttir (1871–1957) and her sisters made the first stairs to the falls, guiding people through formerly impassable terrain. In 1907 foreign investors wanted to dam the Hvítá river, which feeds the falls, for a hydroelectric project. Sigríður's father, Tómas Tómasson, only leased them the land, but the developers got permission from the government. Sigríður walked (barefoot!) to Reykjavík to protest. When the investors failed to pay the lease, the agreement was nullified and the falls escaped destruction. Gullfoss was donated to the nation, and since 1979 it's been a nature reserve. Look for the **memorial** to Sigríður near the foot of the stairs from the visitors centre.

Nearby: The Kjölur Route

Gullfoss is the final stop on traditional Golden Circle tours. You can continue along magnificent Rte F35 beyond the falls (the Kjölur route) for 14.8km while it's paved, after which you need to have a 4WD. Alternatively, take a Highland-routed Reykjavík–Akureyri bus, which stops at the Kerlingarfjöll hiking area as well: Reykjavík Excursions (www.re.is) bus 610 or 610A, or the same service sold by Sterna (www.sterna.is).

Top Tips

▶ On grey, drizzly days, mist can envelop the second drop, making Gullfoss slightly less thrilling.

▶ Don't step over the barriers – they're there not just to protect you, but also the fragile environment.

▶ There's accommodation a few kilometres before the falls at **Hótel Gullfoss** (☑ 486 8979; www.hotelgullfoss.is; d incl breakfast kr20,000; ☜), where clean en-suite rooms overlook the moors (get one facing the valley), and there are two hot-pots and a **restaurant** (mains kr2600 to kr5000) with sweeping views.

Take a Break

Above Gullfoss and next to the main parking lot, the tourist information centre has a basic **cafe** (www.gullfoss.is; mains kr1250-1950; ☺9am-9pm Jun-Aug, to 6.30pm Sep-May; ☜) that sells a well-known lamb soup, and other soups, salads, sandwiches, cakes and coffee.

Hverasvæðið geothermal park (p86)

Experiences

Gamla Laugin   GEOTHERMAL POOL

1 ◎ Map p84, D3

Soak in this broad, calm geothermal pool, mist rising and ringed by natural rocks. The walking trail along the edge of this lovely hot spring passes the local river and a series of sizzling vents and geysers. Surrounding meadows fill with wildflowers in summer. Increasingly popular, the lagoon gets packed with tour bus crowds in mid-afternoon, so come earlier or later.

There's also an on-site coffee shop. Find the lagoon signposted on the northern bank of the river Litla-Laxá in Flúðir. (Secret Lagoon; ☎555 3351; www.secretlagoon.is; Flúðir; adult/child kr2800/free; ⊙10am-10pm May-Sep, noon-8pm Oct-Apr)

Fontana   GEOTHERMAL POOL

2 ◎ Map p84, C2

This swanky lakeside soaking spot boasts three mod wading pools, and a cedar-lined steam room that's fed by a naturally occurring vent below. The cool cafe (buffet lunch/dinner kr2950/4500) has lake views. You can rent towels or swimsuits (kr800 each) if you left yours at home. (☎486 1400; www.fontana.is; Hverabraut 1, Laugarvatn; adult/child kr3800/2000; ⊙10am-11pm early Jun-late Aug, 11am-10pm late Aug-early Jun)

Top Tip

Circle vs Ring

Don't confuse the Golden Circle with the Ring Road (Rte 1), which wraps around the entire country (and takes a week or more to properly complete).

Geothermal Park

HOT SPRINGS

 Map p84, A3

The geothermal park Hverasvæðið, in the centre of town, has mud pots and steaming pools where visitors can dip their feet (but no more). You can book ahead for a guided walk to learn about the area's unique geology and greenhouse power. Or they'll give you an egg and apparatus (kr100) for boiling it in the steaming vents. There's also a small cafe with geothermally baked bread. (Hveragarðurinn; 📞483 4601; Hveramörk 13, Hveragerði; adult/child kr300/free; ⏱9am-6pm Mon-Sat, 10am-4pm Sun Jun-Aug, reduced hours Apr, May & Sep, closed Oct-Mar)

Reykjadalur

GEOTHERMAL POOL

4 ◉ Map p84, A3

Reykjadalur is a delightful geothermal valley where there's a bathable hot river – bring your swimsuit. There are maps at the tourist office to find the trail; from the trailhead car park, it's a 3km hike through fields of sulphur-belching plains. Stick to marked paths, lest you melt your shoes, and leave no rubbish. (Hot River Valley; Hveragerði)

Skálholt

HISTORIC SITE

5 ◉ Map p84, C3

The important religious centre of Skálholt was one of two bishoprics (the other was Hólar in the north) that ruled Iceland's souls from the 11th to the 18th centuries. It rose to prominence under Gissur the White, the driving force behind the Christianisation of Iceland. Today there's a modern Protestant theological centre with a visitor centre, a turf-house recreation of Þorlaksbúð, and a prim church with a museum in the basement containing the stone sarcophagus of Bishop Páll Jónsson (bishop from 1196 to 1211).

Kerið

VOLCANO

6 ◉ Map p84, B3

Around 15.5km north of Selfoss on Rte 35, Kerið is a 6500-year-old explosion crater with vivid red and sienna earth and containing an ethereal green lake. Björk once performed a concert from a floating raft in the middle. (adult/child kr400/free; ⏱8.30am-9pm Jun-Aug, daylight hours Sep-May)

Listasafn Árnesinga

ART MUSEUM

7 ◉ Map p84, A4

This airy modern art gallery puts on great contemporary-art exhibitions, and also has a fine cafe. (📞483 1727; www.listasafnarnesinga.is; Austurmörk 21,

Understand

Supernatural Iceland: Ghosts, Trolls & Hidden People

Once you see the vast lava fields, eerie natural formations and isolated farms that characterise much of the Icelandic landscape, it should come as no surprise that many Icelanders' beliefs go beyond the scientific. It's easy to envision hidden people *(huldufólk)*, ghosts and trolls roaming the landscape and shores.

Hidden People

In the lava are *jarðvergar* (gnomes), *álfar* (elves), *ljósálfar* (fairies), *dvergar* (dwarves), *ljúflingar* (lovelings), *tívar* (mountain spirits) and *englar* (angels). Stories about them have been handed down through generations, and many modern Icelanders claim to have seen these *huldufólk* (hidden people)...or at least to know someone who has.

As in Ireland, there are stories about projects going wrong when workers try to build roads through *huldufólk* homes: the weather turns bad, machinery breaks down, labourers fall ill. In mid-2014 Iceland's 'whimsy factor' again made international news when a road project to link the Álftanes peninsula to the Reykjavík suburb of Garðabær was halted when campaigners warned it would disturb elf habitat.

Ghosts & Trolls

As for Icelandic ghosts, they're substantial beings – not the wafting shadows found elsewhere in Europe. Írafell-Móri (*móri* and *skotta* are used for male and female ghosts, respectively) needed to eat supper every night, and one of the country's most famous spooks, Sel-Móri, got seasick when he stowed away in a boat. Rock stacks and certain lava formations are often said to be trolls, caught out at sunrise and turned forever to stone.

Finding Out More

Surveys suggest that more than half of Icelanders at least entertain the possibility of the existence of *huldufólk*. But a word of warning: many Icelanders get sick of visitors asking, and they don't enjoy the 'Those cute Icelanders! They believe in pixies!' attitude. To ask all the questions you want, join a tour in **Hafnarfjörður**, 10km south of Reykjavík, or take a course at the **Icelandic Elf School** (Álfaskólinn; www.elfmuseum.com) in Reykjavík. Yes, there really is such a place, and it runs four-hour introductory classes most Fridays.

Hveragerði; admission free; ⏱noon-6pm May-Sep, noon-6pm Thu-Sun Oct–mid-Dec & mid-Jan–Apr)

Gljúfrasteinn Laxness Museum
MUSEUM

Nobel Prize–winning author Halldór Laxness (1902–98) lived in Mosfellsbær his whole life. His riverside home is now the Gljúfrasteinn Laxness Museum (off map p84), easy to visit on the road from Reykjavík to Þingvellir (Rte 36). The author built this upper-class 1950s house and it remains intact with original furniture, writing room and Laxness' fine-art collection (needlework, sweetly, by his wife Auður). An audio tour leads you round. Look for his beloved Jaguar parked out the front. (☎586 8066; www.gljufrasteinn. is; Mosfellsbær; adult/child kr900/free; ⏱9am-5pm daily Jun-Aug, 10am-5pm Tue-Sun Mar-May, Sep, Oct & Dec, 10am-5pm Tue-Fri Jan, Feb & Nov)

Laxnes
HORSE RIDING

Small, family-owned Laxnes is run by an older couple whose nephews take newbies out for relaxed trots (two-hour ride kr12,000). On the road from Reykjavík to Þingvellir (off map p84). Also offers combo tours and pickup. (☎566 6179; www.laxnes.is; Mosfellsbær)

Laugarvatn Adventures
ROCK CLIMBING, CAVING

Runs two- to three-hour caving and rock-climbing trips (from kr12,300) in the hills around Laugarvatn (see ② ⊙ Map 84, C2). (☎862 5614; www.caving.is; Laugarvatn)

Eating

Lindin
ICELANDIC $$

Owned by Baldur, an affable, celebrated chef, Lindin is the best restaurant for miles. In a sweet little silver house, the restaurant faces the lake just next to Fontana (see ② ⊙ Map 84,

---

Local Life
Waterways

The Golden Circle offers several prime ways to enjoy local waters.

▸ Scuba dive or snorkel the crystalline Silfra fissure, one of the cracks in the Þingvellir rift valley. Book with **Dive.is** (☎578 6200; www.dive.is; 2 dives at Þingvellir kr45,000) or **Scuba Iceland** (☎892 1923; www.scuba.is; Silfra dive tour with 2 dives kr39,900).

▸ **Arctic Rafting** (☎571 2200; www.arcticrafting.com; ⏱mid-May–mid-Sep) offers tours combining Hvítá river rafting and horse riding, ATV-ing or snowmobiling. Based near Reykholt at Drumboddsstaðir; its Reykjavík office is at Arctic Adventures (p135).

▸ **Iceland Riverjet** (☎863 4506; www.icelandriverjet.com; Skólabraut 4; ⏱mid-Apr–Sep) has jetboat rides along the Hvítá. Based in Reykholt.

C2) and is purely gourmet, with high-concept Icelandic fare featuring local or wild-caught ingredients. The casual, modern bistro serves a more informal menu from soups to an amazing reindeer burger. Book ahead for dinner in high season. (☏ 486 1262; www.laugarvatn.is; Lindarbraut 2, Laugarvatn; restaurant mains kr3800-6300, bistro mains kr2200-5600; ⊗noon-10pm May-Sep, reduced hours Oct-Apr; P 🛜)

Efstidalur II
ICELANDIC $$

8 🍴 Map p84, C2

Located 12km northeast of Laugarvatn on a working dairy farm with brilliant views of hulking Hekla, Efstidalur offers tasty meals and amazing ice cream. The restaurant serves beef from the farm and trout from the lake. The fun ice-cream bar scoops farm ice cream (kr400 per scoop), and has windows looking into the dairy barn. There's also a breakfast buffet (adult/child kr1750/900). (☏ 486 1186; www.efstidalur.is; Efstidalur 2; mains kr2250-5500; ⊗7.30am-9.30am & 11.30am-9pm; P 🛜)

Varmá
ICELANDIC $$$

At the Frost & Fire Hotel in Hveragerði (see 3 Map B4, A3), this wonderfully scenic restaurant boasts floor-to-ceiling windows looking over the stream and gorge. Dishes are Icelandic, using fresh, local ingredients and herbs and often geothermal cooking techniques. Book ahead in summer. (☏ 483 4959; www.frostogfuni.is;

Top Tip

Planning Your Journey

▶ Seeing the Golden Circle with your own vehicle allows you to visit at off-hours and explore attractions further afield.

▶ Visiting with a tour, on the other hand, takes out the guesswork. Almost every tour company in Reykjavík offers a Golden Circle excursion.

▶ If you want to spend the night in the relatively small region, Laugarvatn has good services. Otherwise, camp at Þingvellir, luxe it at **Ion Luxury Adventure Hotel** (☏ 482 3415; www.ioniceland.is; Nesjavellir vid Þingvallavatn; d kr50,100; P @ 🛜 ☒) or choose from accommodation along Rte 35.

▶ To go on to West Iceland afterwards, complete the Circle backwards, finishing with Þingvellir.

Hverhamar, Hveragerði; mains kr4300-6000; ⊗8am-10pm; P 🛜)

Tryggvaskáli
ICELANDIC $$

9 🍴 Map p84, B4

Tryggvaskáli is located in Selfoss' first house (built for bridge workers in 1890). Lovingly renovated and set on the riverfront with a romantic mood, the intimate dining rooms are filled with antique touches, and the fine-dining Icelandic menu sources

Top Tip

Completing the Loop

If you're completing the Golden Circle in the traditional direction, starting at Þingvellir, then the route from Gullfoss back to the Ring Road at **Selfoss** and the geothermal fields at **Hveragerði** will be the final stage of your trip. Along the way you'll find plenty to lure you to stop. Most people follow surfaced Rte 35, which passes through **Reykholt**, with its river rafting. You can also detour slightly to **Flúðir**, with its geothermal greenhouses and hot spring, and **Skálholt**, once Iceland's religious powerhouse.

local produce. The owners also operate Kaffi Krús. (☎ 482 1390; www.tryggvaskali.is; Austurvegur 1, Selfoss; mains kr3300-6000; ◷ 11.30am-10pm Sun-Thu, to 11pm Fri & Sat)

Kaffi Krús
INTERNATIONAL $$

10 Map p84, B4

The 'coffee mug' is a popular cafe in a charming old house along the main road. There's a great outdoor space and a large selection of Icelandic and international dishes from nachos to excellent pizza and burgers. (☎ 482 1266; www.kaffikrus.is; Austurvegur 7, Selfoss; mains kr2000-3600; ◷ 10am-10pm Jun-Aug, reduced hours Sep-May)

Skyrgerðin
CAFE $$

11 Map p84, A3

This chilled-out new cafe incorporates rough wood furniture, antiques and vintage photos to create an interesting environment for dining on creative meals crafted from fresh Icelandic produce. The menu ranges from fresh *skyr*-based smoothies and drinks to sliders, lasagne and fish. There are also pretty little rooms (doubles with/without bathrooms from kr35,000/24,500) upstairs. (☎ 481 1010; Breiðamörk 25, Hveragerði; mains kr2000-2500; ◷ 11am-10pm Mon-Thu, to 11pm Fri-Sun; ☜)

Minilik Ethiopian Restaurant
ETHIOPIAN $$

Sweet-faced Azeb cooks up traditional Ethiopian specialities in this welcoming, unpretentious spot in Flùðir (see 1 Map 84, D3). There are loads of vegetarian options, but also lamb dishes such as *awaze tibs* or chicken (*doro kitfo*). As far as we know, this is the only Ethiopian restaurant in Iceland, and it should beckon all lovers of spice. (☎ 846 9798; www.minilik.is; Flúðir; mains kr2000-3000; ◷ noon-9pm Jun-Aug, 6-9pm Sep-May; ☝)

Café Mika
INTERNATIONAL $$

12 Map p84, D2

Café Mika is popular with locals for its huge menu, outdoor pizza oven, sandwiches and Icelandic mains.

Turf-house recreation at Skálholt (p86)

(📞896 6450; Skólabraut 4, Reykholt; mains kr1900-6000; ⏰noon-9pm; 🛜)

Grund Restaurant ICELANDIC $$
This popular restaurant in Flùðir (see 1 🗺 Map 84, D3) serves fresh local food in a large, cheerful dining room. (📞565 9196; www.gistingfludir.is; Flúðir; mains kr2600-4900; ⏰11.30am-9pm Jun–mid-Aug)

Shopping
Gallerí Laugarvatn ARTS & CRAFTS
Local handicrafts, from ironwork to ceramics and woollens, are to be found at this gallery in Laugarvatn (see 2 🗺 Map 84, C2). Also operates a small B&B and offers courses. (📞847 0805; www.gallerilaugarvatn.is; Háholt 1, Laugarvatn; ⏰1-6pm mid-May–mid-Sep, 1-6pm Sat & Sun mid-Sep–mid-May)

Explore

South Coast

The Ring Road (Rte 1) sweeps southeast of Reykjavík through wide coastal plains before the landscape grows wonderfully jagged, after Hvolsvöllur and Hella, near Skógar and Vík. Inland, mountains thrust upwards, some of them volcanoes wreathed by mist (such as Eyjafjalla-jökull, pictured above during the 2010 eruption), and awesome glaciers glimmer, as rivers carve their way to black-sand beaches.

The Region in a Day

 The South Coast is enormous, so you'll need to pick your focus. Head east along the Ring Road, stopping near Hella or Hvolsvöllur for **horse riding** (p97), saga studies at **Sögusetrið** (p100) and volcanic studies at **LAVA – Iceland Volcano & Earthquake Center** (p98). Or hit the coast at **Stokkseyri and Eyrarbakki** for a taste of local life in an Icelandic fishing village. Or, plan a day trip to the **Vestmannaeyjar Islands**.

Lunch at **Gamla Fjósið** (p101) and stop off at **Eyjafjalla-jökull Visitor Centre** (p100); or head straight along to Skógar, stopping at the several grand **waterfalls** (p96), the **Skógar Folk Museum** (p98) and **Sólheimajökull** (p97) ice tongue. Take any number of adventure tours, or zip along to Vík's magnificent coastline at **Dyrhólaey** (p96) and **Reynisfjara** (p96).

In summer book ahead for dinner at Vík's **Suður-Vík** (p101) or drop in to **Halldórskaffi** (p102). Definitely reserve ahead to spend the night and see more of this popular part of the country, or power back to Reykjavík.

 Best of South Coast

Natural Wonders
Vatnajökull (p103)

Sólheimajökull (p97)

Seljalandsfoss (p96)

Skógafoss (p98)

Hekla (p99)

Eyjafjallajökull (p100)

Eldfell (p99)

Svartifoss (p103)

Eating
Slippurinn (p102)

Getting There

🚗 **Car** Gives the most freedom; roads are good except deep inland.

⊚ **Tours** Almost all Reykjavík-based tour companies offer excursions to the south, and many local operators can also pick up in Reykjavík.

🚌 **Bus** The most popular tourist routes in the country head through here. All companies – Strætó (p147), Sterna (p147) and Reykjavík Excursions (p147) – offer myriad lines. Trex (p147) serves Þórsmörk and Landmannalaugar.

A Kerlingarfjöll (45km)

Bjarnarfell (727m)

Geysir

Gullfoss

B

C

D

35 Brúarhlöð

358 30

F26

Þórisvatn

Háifoss

Sultartangalón

Litlisjór

Veidivötn

F235

Bláskógar Hydroelectric Plant

Flúðir

Þjóðveldisbærinn 32

26

Hjálparfoss

Þjórsá

Búrfell (669m)

F225

Fjallabak Nature Reserve

4WD only

F208

Árnes

Leirubakki

Landmannalaugar

Jökuldalur

Lakagígar

F208

26

Yfri-Ranga

272

268

Hekla (1491m)

Laufafell

Kirkjufell

Eldgjá

Gjátindu

Árbakki

Vatnafjöll

Torfajökull

271

Hella

264

Keldur F210

8

Álftavatn

F208

264

Fljótsdalur

F210

7 LAVA - Iceland Volcano & Earthquake Center

Tindfjallajökull

Eyrabakki & Stokkseyri (45km)

Hvolsvöllur

Hlíðarendi

261

Tindfjöll (1251m)

Þórsmörk

F261

255

Stóra-Mörk III

Valahnúkur (282m)

Mýrdalsjökull

Mýrdalsjökull

209

3

Bergþórshvoll

Seljalandsfoss & Gljúfurárbúi

Eyjafjallajökull

Fimmvörðuháls

253

Katla (1250m)

Hafursey (582m)

1

Bakki 247 Ásólfsskáli

1

9 10 Seljavallalaug

Skógafoss

Landeyjahöfn

Eyjafjallajökull Visitor Centre

Skógar

6 221 4 Sólheimajökull

5 Skógar Folk Museum

Mælifell (642m)

Mýrdalssandur

219 Brekkur

11

Hjörleifshöfði (221m)

Heimaey

1 Vík

Vestmannaeyjar

Dyrhólaey

2 Reynisfjara

12

5

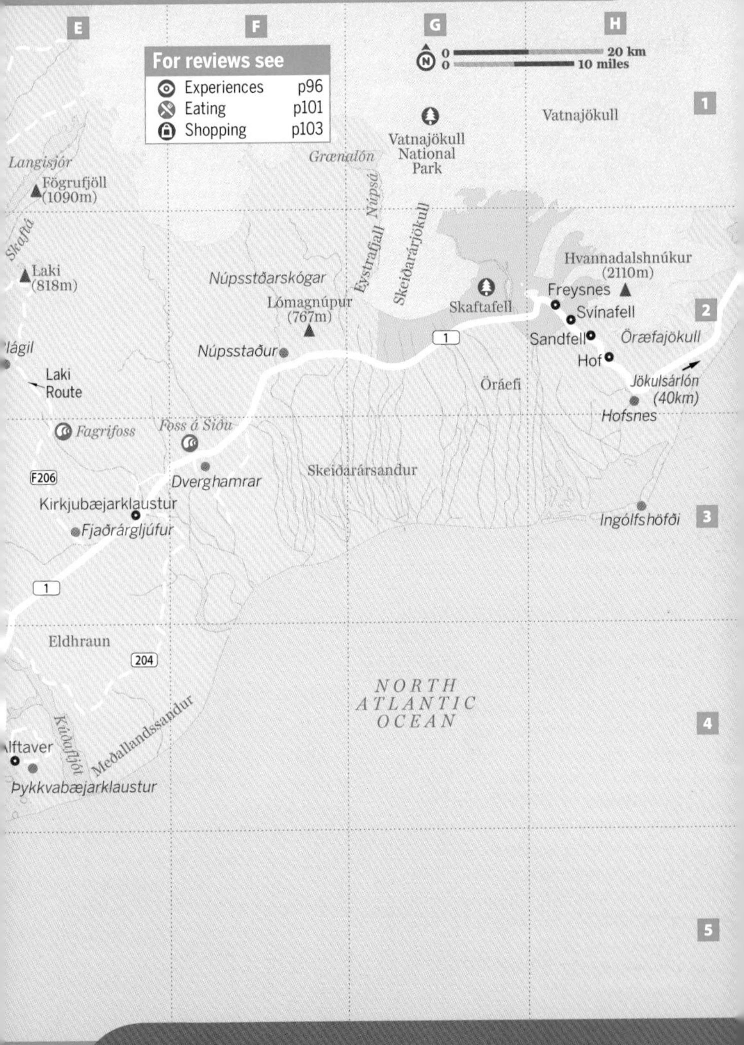

E   F   G   H

For reviews see
- Experiences   p96
- Eating   p101
- Shopping   p103

N   0 _____ 20 km
    0 _____ 10 miles

Langisjór

▲Fögrufjöll
(1090m)

Grænalón

Vatnajökull

Vatnajökull
National
Park

Skaftá

▲Laki
(818m)

Núpsstðarskógar

Lómagnúpur
(767m)
▲

Skaftafell

Hvannadalshnúkur
(2110m)
Freysnes ▲
Svínafell
Sandfell
Hof

Öræfajökull

Eystrafjall *Núpsá* *Skeiðará* *Skeiðarárjökull*

1

...lágil

Laki
Route

Núpsstaður

Jökulsárlón
(40km)

Öræfi

Hofsnes

Fagrifoss

Foss á Síðu

F206

Kirkjubæjarklaustur

Dverghamrar

Skeiðarársandur

Ingólfshöfði

3

Fjaðrárgljúfur

1

Eldhraun

204

NORTH
ATLANTIC
OCEAN

4

Kúðafljót *Meðallandssandur*

...alftaver

Þykkvabæjarklaustur

5

Experiences

Reynisfjara
BEACH

1 Map p94, C5

On the west side of Reynisfjall, the high ridge above Vík, Rte 215 leads 5km down to black-sand beach Reynisfjara. It's backed by an incredible stack of **basalt columns** that look

like a magical church organ, and there are outstanding views west to Dyrhólaey. Surrounding cliffs are pocked with caves formed from twisted basalt, and puffins belly flop into the crashing sea during summer. Immediately offshore are the towering **Reynisdrangur** sea stacks. At all times watch for rogue waves: people are regularly swept away.

Dyrhólaey
WILDLIFE RESERVE

2 Map p94, C5

One of the Couth Coast's most recognisable natural formations is the rocky plateau and huge stone sea arch at Dyrhólaey (deer-lay), which rises dramatically from the surrounding plain 10km west of Vík, at the end of Rte 218. Visit its crashing black beaches and get awesome views from atop the promontory. The islet is a nature reserve that's rich in bird life, including puffins; some or all of it can be closed during nesting season (15 May to 25 June).

Seljalandsfoss & Gljúfurárbui
WATERFALL

3 Map p94, A4

From the Ring Road you'll see the beautiful high falls at Seljalandsfoss, which tumble over a rocky scarp into a deep, green pool. A (slippery) path runs around the back of the waterfall. A few hundred metres further down the Þórsmörk road, Gljúfurárbui gushes into a hidden canyon.

Q **Local Life**

Stokkseyri & Eyrarbakki

South of the Ring Road the tiny fishing villages of Stokkseyri and Eyrarbakki are refreshingly local-feeling. Stokkseyri has summertime art galleries and **Draugasetrið** (Ghost Centre; ☎ 483 1202; www.draugasetrid.is; Hafnargata 9; adult/child kr2000/1000, incl Icelandic Wonders kr3500/1500; ☉ 1-6pm Jun-Aug), a veritable haunted house run by a gaggle of bloodthirsty teens. Eyrarbakki's **Flói Nature Reserve** is super for birdwatching, and **Húsið á Eyrarbakka** (House at Eyrarbakki; ☎ 483 1504; www.husid.com; Hafnarbrú 3; adult/child incl Sjóminjasafnið á Eyrarbakka kr1000/free; ☉ 11am-6pm mid-May–mid-Sep) is one of Iceland's oldest houses. Duelling restaurants **Við Fjöruborðið** (☎ 483 1550; www.fjorubordid.is; Eyrarbraut 3a; mains kr3200-6000; ☉ noon-9pm Jun-Aug, 5-9pm Sep-May; ☎) and **Rauða Húsið** (☎ 483 3330; www.raudahusid.is; Búðarstígur 4; mains kr3000-6000; ☉ 11.30am-10pm Jun-Aug, reduced hours Sep-May; ☎) contend for the 'best lobster bisque' award.

Svartifoss waterfall, Vatnajökull National Park (p103)

Sólheimajökull

GLACIER

4 ⊙ Map p94, C4

One of the easiest glacial tongues to reach is Sólheimajökull. This icy outlet glacier unfurls from the main Mýrdalsjökull ice cap and is a favourite spot for glacial walks and ice climbing. Rte 221 leads 4.2km off the Ring Road to a small car park and the **Arcanum Glacier Café** (Café Solheimajökull; ☎547 1500; www.arcanum.is; snacks kr750-1375; ⏰9.30am-5pm May-Sep, reduced hours Oct-Apr; 🛜), from where you can walk the 800m to the ice along a wide track edging the glacial lagoon. Don't attempt to climb onto the glacier unguided.

Local Life
Horse Riding

Many horse farms around the south, especially near Hella and Hvolsvöllur, and between Skógar and Vík, offer rides or multiday tours, and most have accommodation. Expect to pay kr6500 to kr9000 for a one-hour ride to kr30,000 for a day-long ride, though prices can drop for groups. Outfitters include **Herríðarhóll** (☎487 5252; www.herridarholl.is; Herríðarhóli), **Sólhestar** (☎892 3066; www.solhestar.is; Borgargerði, Ölfus) and **Skálakot** (☎487 8953; www.skalakot.com).

Skógar Folk Museum   MUSEUM

5 ⊙ Map p94, B4

The highlight of little Skógar is the wonderful Skógar Folk Museum, which covers all aspects of Icelandic life. The vast collection was put

Top Tip

Adventure Tours

South Iceland is the land of adventure tours. Most local operators offer lots of combinations and Reykjavík pick-ups; most Reykjavík companies also run tours here.

▶ **Midgard Adventure** (☑770 2030; www.midgardadventure.is; Dufþaksbraut 14) Great bespoke adventure operators: hiking, super-Jeeps, canyoning, ice climbing.

▶ **Southcoast Adventure** (☑867 3535; www.southadventure.is) Excellent small operator with super-Jeeps, hiking, snowmobiling, volcano tours and glacier walks.

▶ **Icelandic Mountain Guides** (☑587 9999, Skógar desk ☑894 2956; www.mountainguides.is; ⊙9am-6pm) Sólheimajökull glacier walks and ice climbs.

▶ **Arcanum** (☑487 1500; www.arcanum.is) Daily Sólheimajökull glacier walks, ice climbing, super-Jeep, ATV and other tours.

▶ **Katla Track** (☑849 4404; www.katlatrack.is) Explores landmarks near Vík and Mýrdalsjökull.

together by 95-year-old Þórður Tómasson over more than 75 years. There are also restored buildings – a church, a turf-roofed farmhouse, cowsheds – and a huge, modern building that houses an interesting transport and communication museum, the basic cafe **Skógakaffi** (www.skogasafn.is; soup kr1600; ⊙10am-5pm) and a shop. (Skógasafn; ☑487 8845; www.skogasafn.is; adult/child kr2000/free; ⊙9am-6pm Jun-Aug, 10am-5pm Sep-May)

Skógafoss   WATERFALL

6 ⊙ Map p94, B4

This 62m-high waterfall topples over a rocky cliff at the western edge of Skógar in dramatic style. Climb the steep staircase alongside for giddy views, or walk to the foot of the falls, shrouded in sheets of mist and rainbows. Legend has it that a settler named Þrasi hid a chest of gold behind Skógafoss...

LAVA – Iceland Volcano & Earthquake Center   EXHIBITION

7 ⊙ Map p94, A3

The new LAVA Center opens in summer 2017 with a full-blown multimedia experience immersing you in Iceland's volcanic and seismic life, and includes a 12m-high model of Iceland's volcanic core, an earthquake simulator and a cinema. Its LAVA House is an information centre for the region with a shop and restaurant. (www.lavacentre.is; Austurvegur 14, Hvolsvöllur; adult/child kr2600/free, cinema only kr1200/free; ⊙exhibition 10am-7pm, LAVA house 9am-10pm)

Understand
Icelandic Volcanoes

Situated on the Mid-Atlantic Ridge, a massive 18,000km-long rift between two of the earth's major tectonic plates, Iceland is a shifting, steaming lesson in classroom geology. A mere baby in geological terms, Iceland is the youngest country in Europe, formed by underwater volcanic eruptions along the joint of the North American and Eurasian plates 17 to 20 million years ago. The earth's crust in Iceland is only a third of its normal thickness, and magma (molten rock) continues to rise from deep within, forcing the two plates apart. The result is clearly visible at **Þingvellir**, where the great rift Almannagjá broadens by between 1mm and 18mm per year.

The thin crust and grating plates are responsible for a whole host of exciting volcanic activities, but fissure eruptions and their associated craters are probably the most common type of eruption in Iceland. The still-volatile Lakagígar crater row around **Mt Laki** is the country's most unearthly example. It produced the largest lava flow in human history in the 18th century, covering an area of 565 sq km to a depth of 12m.

Subglacial & Submarine Eruptions
Several of Iceland's liveliest volcanoes lie beneath glaciers, which makes for drama as molten lava and ice interact. The eruption of **Eyjafjallajökull** in 2010 caused a *jökulhlaup* (flooding caused by volcanic eruption beneath an ice cap) before throwing up the famous ash plume that grounded Europe's aeroplanes. Iceland's most active volcano, **Grímsvötn**, which lies beneath Vatnajökull ice cap, behaved similarly in 2011.

In 1963 the island of **Surtsey** exploded from the sea, giving scientists the opportunity to study how smouldering chunks of newly created land are colonised by plants and animals. Surtsey is off-limits to visitors, but you can climb many classical-looking cones such as **Hekla**, once thought to be the gateway to Hell; **Eldfell**, which did its best to bury the town of Heimaey in 1974; and **Snæfellsjökull** on the Snæfellsnes Peninsula.

The **Icelandic Met Office** (www.vedur.is) keeps track of eruptions and the earthquakes that tend to precede them, plus the emissions that follow.

Sögusetrið
MUSEUM

Hvolsvöllur's Saga Centre (see 7
Map 94, A3) is devoted to the dramatic
events of *Njál's Saga,* which took
place in the surrounding hills.
Interactive displays explain the many
highlights of the story. In 2013 an
intricate 90m embroidery called **Njál's
Saga Tapestry** was begun; visitors can
pay to add stitches to the enormous
collaborative project (kr1000; check
www.njalurefill.is for the sewing
schedule), or just observe. There's
also an art exhibition, a longhouse
coffee shop and tourist information
(brochures, maps and helpful staff).
(Saga Centre; ☑ 487 8781; www.njala.is;
Hliðarvegur 14, Hvolsvöllur; adult/child kr900/
free; ⊘ 9am-6pm mid-May–mid-Sep, 10am-
5pm Sat & Sun mid-Sep–mid-May)

Keldur
RUINS

8 ⊙ Map p94, A3

About 5km west of Hvolsvöllur, unsur-
faced Rte 264 winds about 8km north
along the Rangárvellir valley to the
medieval turf-roofed farm at Keldur.
This historic settlement once belonged
to Ingjaldur Höskuldsson, a character
in *Njál's Saga.* The structure is man-
aged by the National Museum Historic
Buildings Collection and has interesting historical exhibits and a pastoral
setting. (☑ 530 2200; www.thjodminjasafn.
is; kr750; ⊘ 10am-5pm mid-Jun–mid-Aug)

Eyjafjallajökull
Visitor Centre
EXHIBITION

9 ⊙ Map p94, B4

This centre, about 7km west of Skógar
on the Ring Road, is on a farm on the

Understand
Landmannalaugar & Þórsmörk Trekking

Mind-blowing multicoloured rhyolite mountains, soothing hot springs, ram-
bling lava flows and clear blue lakes make **Landmannalaugar** one of Iceland's
most unique destinations. The area is the starting point for the famous multiday **Laugavegurinn hike**, and there's some excellent day hiking as well. The
popular 55km Laugavegurinn leads south to the hidden valley of **Þórsmörk**
(thors-mork, literally Thor's forest) at the dramatic confluence of several
larger river-carved valleys. A nature reserve, Þórsmörk is a verdant realm of
forest and flower-filled lees that looks onto curling gorges, icy rivers, and three
looming glaciers (Tindfjallajökull, Eyjafjallajökull and Mýrdalsjökull). Its lovely
setting and proximity to Reykjavík (130km) make it a popular spot in summer.
Þórsmörk may seem relatively close to the Ring Road on a map (and it is the
better destination for those short on time), but you'll need to take a bus or go
by high-clearance 4WD (super-Jeep tour!) to ford the rivers on the way to the
reserve. Or hike in on the Fimmvörðuháls trail from Skógar.

southern flanks of Eyjafjallajökull that was impacted by the 2010 eruption. A 20-minute film (usually in English) tells the family's story, from the ominous warnings to the devastating aftermath of the flooding ash. Movie snippets include tender family moments and highlights from the team of local rescuers that dug the farm out. (Þorvaldseyri Visitor Center – Iceland Erupts; ☎487 8815; www.icelanderupts.is; Þorvaldseyri; adult/child kr800/free; ⏱9am-6pm Jun-Aug, 10am-4pm May & Sep, 11am-4pm Mon-Fri Oct-Apr)

Seljavallalaug   GEOTHERMAL POOL

 10 Map p94, B4

Seljavallalaug, a peaceful pool built in 1923, is filled by a natural hot spring and has become very popular with tourists. From Edinborg (7km west of Skógar) follow Rte 242 and signs 2km to Seljavellir; park by the farm, and walk up the beautiful river valley for about 10 minutes. (admission free)

Eating

Suður-Vík   ICELANDIC, ASIAN $$

 11 Map p94, C4

The friendly ambience, from hardwood floors and interesting artwork to smiling staff, helps elevate this restaurant beyond the competition. Food is Icelandic hearty, from heaping steak sandwiches with bacon and Béarnaise sauce, to Asian (think Thai satay with

JAN MASTNIK / SHUTTERSTOCK ©

Seljavallalaug

rice). In a warmly lit silver building atop town. Book ahead in summer. (☎487 1515; www.facebook.com/Sudurvik; Suðurvíkurvegur 1, Vík; mains kr2100-5000; ⏱noon-10pm)

Gamla Fjósið   ICELANDIC $$

Built in a former cowshed that was in use until 1999, this charming eatery's focus is on farm-fresh and grass-fed meaty mains – from burgers to Volcano Soup, a spicy meat stew. The hardwood floor and low beams are cheered with polished dining tables, large wooden hutches and friendly staff. It's just down the road from the Eyjafjallajökull Visitor Centre (see 9 Map 94, B4). (Old Cowhouse; ☎487 7788;

www.gamlafjosid.is; Hvassafell; mains kr1900-6500; ⏰11am-9pm Jun-Aug, reduced hours Sep-May; 🛜)

Halldórskaffi   INTERNATIONAL $$

Inside Vík's Brydebúð museum (see 11 ❌ Map 94, C4), this lively all-rounder is very popular in high season for its crowd-pleasing menu ranging from burgers and pizza to lamb fillet. Be prepared to wait in summer since it doesn't take reservations. Weekend nights it stays open later as a bar. (📞487 1202; www.halldorskaffi.is; Víkurbraut 28, Vík; mains kr2000-5000; ⏰11am-10pm Jun-Aug, reduced hours Sep-May)

Local Life
Vestmannaeyjar

Vestmannaeyjar (or Westman Islands) form 15 eye-catching silhouettes off the shore. **Heimaey** (map p94, A4) is the only inhabited island, and its town lies between escarpments and volcanoes (part of a 1973 eruption that almost covered the village). Heimaey is famous for its 10 million puffins, the Þjóðhátíð festival and its excellent museum, **Eldheimar** (Pompeii of the North; 📞488 2700; www.eldheimar.is; Gerðisbraut 10; adult/child kr2300/1200; ⏰10.30am-6pm May–mid-Oct, 1-5pm Wed-Sun mid-Oct–Apr). It's a great day trip on the Herjólfur ferry. **Slippurinn** (📞481 1515; www.slippurinn. com; Strandvegur 76; mains lunch kr 2200-3000, dinner mains kr3500-4000; ⏰noon-2.30pm & 5-10pm early May–mid-Sep; 🛜) serves top meals.

Hótel Skógafoss Bistro-Bar   ICELANDIC $$

The bistro-bar at Hótel Skógafoss in Skógar (see 5 ◉ Map 94, B4) is one of the best eating and drinking spots in town, with plate-glass windows looking onto the falls and local beer on tap. (📞487 8780; www.hotelskogafoss. is; Skógar; mains kr1600-2500; ⏰8am-11pm Jun-Sep, to 10pm Oct-May)

Svarta Fjaran   CAFE $$

12 ❌ Map p94, C5

Black volcanic cubes meant to mimic the nearby black beach Reynisfjara with its famous basalt columns, house this contemporary restaurant that serves homemade cakes and snacks during the day and a full dinner menu at night. Plate-glass windows give views to the ocean and Dyrhólaey beyond. (Black Beach Restaurant; 📞571 2718; www.svartafjaran.com; Reynisfjara; snacks kr990, dinner mains kr2500-6000; ⏰11am-10pm; 🛜)

Eldstó Art Café   CAFE $$

Eldstó (see 7 ◉ Map 94, A3) offers fresh-brewed coffee, daily homemade specials (such as coconut curry soup), and some outdoor Ring Road–side tables. Friendly owners are ceramicists with a small on-site gallery, and also offer simple accommodation upstairs (doubles from kr28,000). (📞482 1011; www.eldsto.is; Austurvegur 2, Hvolsvöllur; mains kr2000-4000; ⏰11am-9.30pm Jun-Aug; 🅿🛜)

Understand
Skaftafell & Vatnajökull National Park

Vatnajökull National Park (www.vjp.is; www.visitvatnajokull.is) is the largest park in Europe, measuring 13,900 sq km – nearly 14% of the entire country. Skaftafell, the jewel in the park's crown, encompasses a breathtaking collection of peaks and glaciers. It's Iceland's favourite wilderness: 300,000 visitors per year come to marvel at thundering waterfalls, twisted birch woods, tangled rivers threading across the *sandar*, and brilliant blue-white Vatnajökull with its enormous ice tongues. There are around 30 of these outlet glaciers, pleated with crevasses, with many visible (and accessible, to varying degrees) from the Ring Road in the southeast.

Great year-round **Skaftafellsstofa visitor centre** (☎ 470 8300; www.vjp.is; ⏲9am-7pm May-Sep, 10am-5pm Feb-Apr, Oct & Nov, 11am-5pm Dec, 10am-4pm Jan; 🛜) has exhibitions and a small cafe, and information on walks, like the 1.8km one to **Svartifoss** (Black Falls), a stunning, moody-looking waterfall flanked by geometric black basalt columns. **Icelandic Mountain Guides** (IMG; ☎ Reykjavík 587 9999, Skaftafell 894 2959; www.mountainguides.is; ⏲8.30am-6pm May-Sep, reduced hours Oct-Apr) and **Glacier Guides** (☎ Reykjavík 562 7000, Skaftafell 659 7000; www.glacierguides.is; ⏲8.30am-6pm Apr-Oct, reduced hours Nov-Mar) lead glacier walks and adventure tours.

Ströndin Bistro INTERNATIONAL $$

Behind the N1 petrol station in Vík (see 11 ⊗ Map 94, C4) is this semi-smart wood-panelled option enjoying sea-stack vistas. Go local with lamb soup or fish stew, or global with pizzas and burgers. (☎ 487 1230; www.strondin.is; Austurvegur 18, Vík; mains kr2000-5000; ⏲6-10pm; 🛜)

Shopping

Una Local Products ARTS & CRAFTS

This large hangar on the Ring Road in Hvolsvöllur (see 7 ⊚ Map 94, A3) is loaded with all manner of hand-made Icelandic crafts, from fish-skin purses to woolly jumpers, jewellery and leather goods. (Sveitabúðin Una; ☎ 544 5455; Austurvegur 4, Hvolsvöllur; ⏲10am-6pm; 🛜)

Víkurprjón GIFTS & SOUVENIRS

The big Icewear souvenir and knit-wear shop next to the N1 station in Vík (see 11 ⊗ Map 94, C4) is a coach-tour hit. You can peek inside the factory portion to see woollen wear being made. (☎ 487 1250; www.vikwool.is; Austurvegur 20, Vík; ⏲8am-7pm)

Top Experiences
Jökulsárlón

Getting There

🚗 **Car** Makes over-nighting easy.

🚌 **Bus** Plentiful tours, plus Reykjavík–Höfn Sterna summer bus 12/12a and Strætó bus 51. Also scheduled summer buses from Skaftafell.

One of Iceland's most magical sights, Jökulsárlón glacier lagoon is filled with spectacular, luminous-blue icebergs drifting out to sea. The hours will zip by as you're wowed by wondrous ice sculptures (some striped with ash from volcanic eruptions) as they spin in the changing light, or go scouting for seals or take a boat trip. The icebergs calve from Breiðamerkurjökull glacier, an offshoot of Vatnajökull ice cap. Though it's right beside the Ring Road (between Skaftafell and Höfn), Jökulsárlón is 375km from Reykjavík (4½ hours one way), so warrants sleeping over in the south.

The Lagoon

Although it looks as though it's been here since the last ice age, the lagoon is only about 80 years old. Until the mid-1930s Breiðamerkurjökull reached the Ring Road; it's now retreating rapidly (up to a staggering 500m per year), and the lagoon is growing. Icebergs can spend up to five years floating in the 25-sq-km-plus, 260m-deep lagoon before they travel via Jökulsá, Iceland's shortest river, out to sea.

Boat Tours

Take a memorable 40-minute trip with **Glacier Lagoon Amphibious Boat Tours** (⊘478 2222; www.icelagoon.is; adult/child kr5000/1500; ⊘9am-7pm Jun-Aug, 10am-5pm Apr, May, Sep & Oct), which trundle along the shore like buses before driving into the water. It also offers Zodiac tours, as does **Ice Lagoon Zodiac Boat Tours** (⊘860 9996; www.icelagoon.com; adult/child kr9500/6000; ⊘9am-5.30pm mid-May–mid-Sep), which speed up to the glacier edge (not done by the amphibious boats) before cruising back slowly. Check online for details and to book ahead.

Wildlife

Keep a lookout for seals bobbing up in the lagoon between the brilliant bergs. The zooming Arctic terns nest not only on the shore but also on some of the larger ice chunks!

The River Mouth

Visit the river mouth where you'll see ice boulders resting photogenically on the black-sand beach as part of their final journey out to sea.

admission free

⊘24hr

☑ Top Tips

▶ Summer nights can be glowing golden, and without the tour-bus crowds.

▶ On the Ring Road west of the car park, parking areas have trails to less-touristed shoreline.

▶ Amphibious boat tours generally run April to October; the small cafe here is open year-round.

▶ Restroom facilities are inadequate.

✗ Take a Break

The **cafe** (snacks kr400-2000; ⊘9am-7pm) beside the lagoon has snacks (and long queues).

Þórbergssetur (⊘478 1078; www.thorbergur.is; Hali; adult/child kr1000/free; ⊘9am-8pm), a museum and cultural centre 12km east of the lagoon, has a quality cafe-restaurant.

Explore

West Iceland

Geographically close to Reykjavík yet far, far away in sentiment, West Iceland (Vesturland; www.west.is) is a splendid microcosm of what Iceland has to offer. Snæfellsjökull National Park is great for birding, whale watching, lava field hikes and horse riding. An exceptional museum in lively Borgarnes illustrates local sagas. Upcountry beyond Reykholt you'll encounter lava tubes and remote highland glaciers.

The Region in a Day

☀ Spend your morning in Borgarnes learning about Iceland's Viking settlers and wild, wonderful *Egil's Saga* at the **Settlement Centre** (p108), and touring the local saga sites like **Egil's farm** (p109). Lunch at the Settlement Centre's excellent on-site **restaurant** (p119) or stroll to waterfront cafe **Englendingavík** (p121) for casual eats and great views.

☀ Next, either head inland to take a tour on enormous **Langjökull** (p113), a dip at new spa **Krauma** (p116), or explore Iceland's largest lava tube **Viðgelmir** (p115). Or zip up the coast to the Snæfellsnes Peninsula to spend your afternoon exploring the **National Park** (p110) and going puffin spotting and whale watching on **Breiðafjörður** (p115).

🌙 Overnight in Stykkishólmur for its top lodgings, and restaurants such as **Narfeyrarstofa** (p119), **Plássið** (p120) and **Sjávarpakkhúsið** (p120). Visit interesting museums such as **Norska Húsið** (p116) the next day, or catch some theatre at funky **Freezer Hostel** (p122) before heading back to Reykjavík.

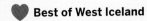

👁 Top Experiences

Settlement Centre (p108)

Snæfellsjökull National Park (p110)

♥ Best of West Iceland

Eating

Bjargarsteinn Mathús (p118)

Narfeyrarstofa (p119)

Natural Wonders

Langjökull (p113)

Snæfellsjökull (p111)

Viðgelmir – the Cave (p115)

Vatnshellir (p111)

Krauma (p116)

Getting There

🚗 **Car** Easiest.

🚌 **Bus** Borgarnes is the major transfer point between Reykjavík and Akureyri, Snæfellsnes and the Westfjords. Strætó (p147) bus 57 stops en route to/from Reykjavík and Akureyri. Bus 58 goes to Stykkishólmur; you can change to bus 82 (Stykkishólmur–Arnarstapi) at the Vatnaleið crossroads to go to western Snæfellsnes. Bus 81 serves Reykholt. Sterna (p147) bus 60/60a and Reykjavík Excursions (p147) bus 320 serve parts of the West.

Top Experiences
Settlement Centre

Borgarnes and its broad Borgarfjörður were the landing zone for several famous Icelandic settlers. Housed in a restored warehouse by the harbour, the fascinating Settlement Centre offers insights into the history of Icelandic settlement and brings alive the story of one of its most famous settlers, poet-warrior Egil Skallagrímsson (the man behind *Egil's Saga*), his amazing adventures and his equally intense family.

Map p114, B4

Landnámssetur Íslands

437 1600

www.settlementcentre.is

Brákarbraut 13-15

10am-9pm

Wood carving of a character from *Egil's Saga*

Settlement Exhibition

The *Settlement Exhibition* vividly covers the discovery and settlement of Iceland and gives a firm historical context in which to place your Icelandic visit. The interactive map illustrating where the first settlers made inroads is particularly fun, and the audioguide's recounting of settlers' stories illustrates how harsh it all was.

Egil's Saga Exhibition

Egil's Saga is one of the most nuanced and action-packed of the sagas, and the exhibition uses creative art and diorama displays to recount how poet-warrior Egil Skallagrímsson's family settled the Borgarnes area, and how Egil became both a fierce and sensitive man, from his near murder by his own father, to the death of his own sons.

Local Landmarks

To explore how *Egil's Saga* ties to the Borgarnes area, download the detailed **Locatify SmartGuide** app. It tells stories of local landmarks which the Settlement Centre has marked with cairns, including **Brákin**, Egil's farm Borg á Mýrum, and **Skallagrímsgarður**, the burial mound of Egil's father and son.

Egil's Farm

Borg á Mýrum (Rock in the Marshes; Rte 54; admission free), just northwest of Borgarnes on Rte 54, is where Skallagrímur Kveldúlfsson, Egil's father, made his farm at Settlement. Named for the large rock (*borg*) behind the farmstead (private property), you can walk up to the **cairn**, for super views. The small **cemetery** includes an ancient rune-inscribed gravestone. Ásmundur Sveinsson's **sculpture** represents Egil mourning the death of his sons and his rejuvenation in poetry.

GARY LATHAM/LONELY PLANET ©

☑ **Top Tips**

▶ The museum is divided into two exhibitions; each takes about 30 minutes to visit. The cost for one exhibition is kr1900 and for two is kr2500.

▶ Kids under 14 are free.

▶ Detailed multi-lingual audioguides are included.

▶ Leave time to explore area sites from *Egil's Saga*.

▶ In summer, reserve ahead for dinner at the Settlement Centre restaurant.

✖ **Take a Break**

The Settlement Centre has a top-notch restaurant (p119) built into the rock face and serving modern Icelandic fare.

If you feel like strolling the town, the fun waterfront Englendingavík (p121) offers a more casual cafe vibe with great water views.

Top Experiences
Snæfellsjökull National Park

Sparkling fjords, dramatic volcanic peaks, sheer sea cliffs, sweeping golden beaches and crunchy lava flows make up the diverse and fascinating landscape of the 100km-long Snæfellsnes Peninsula. The area is crowned by the glistening ice cap Snæfellsjökull, immortalised in Jules Verne's *Journey to the Centre of the Earth* (1864). Snæfellsjökull National Park encompasses much of the peninsula's western tip. You'll find lava tubes, protected lava fields home to native Icelandic fauna, and prime coastal bird- and whale-watching spots.

 Map p112, B3

📞 436 6860

www.snaefellsjokull.is

Sea stacks in winter

Malarrif Visitor Centre & Hikes

Hiking trails criss-cross the park, and the **visitor centre** (Snæfellsjökull National Park Visitor Centre; ☎436 6888, 591 2000; www.snaefellsjokull.is; Malarrif; admission free; ☷10am-5pm Jun-Sep, 10am-4pm Mon-Fri Oct-May; 🛜) in Malarrif sells maps (free online) and gives advice (as do area tourist offices). Rangers have summer programs of free guided tours.

Snæfellsjökull

It's easy to see why Jules Verne chose Snæfell for his adventure *Journey to the Centre of the Earth:* the peak was torn apart when the volcano beneath exploded. Today the crater is filled with the ice cap (highest point 1446m; *jökull* means 'glacier'). To reach its summit take a tour from Hellnar or Arnarstapi; some operators pick up in Reykjavík.

Öndverðarnes

At the westernmost tip of Snæfellsnes an ancient lava flow leads to Öndverðarnes Peninsula, great for **whale watching**. From the last parking area (at a squat, orange lighthouse), walk to the tip of the peninsula, or head 200m northeast to **Fálki**, an ancient stone well thought to have three waters: fresh, holy and ale! The **Svörtuloft bird cliffs** (Saxhólsbjarg) are to the south.

Djúpalón Beach & Dritvík

On the southwest coast, wild black-sand beach **Djúpalónssandur** offers dramatic walks with rock formations (an elf church, and a **kerling** – a troll woman), shipwreck debris and the rock-arch **Gatklettur**. Rocky **sea stacks** emerge from the ocean as you tramp north over the craggy headland to reach black-sand **Dritvík**, once the largest Icelandic fishing station, now lonely ruins.

ANNA MORGAN / SHUTTERSTOCK ©

☑ Top Tips

▶ Good roads (and buses) mean that Snæfellsnes is an easy trip from Reykjavík.

▶ Dress warmly and wear hiking boots and gloves if you're taking a 45-minute guided tour of the fascinating **Vatnshellir Lava Cave.**

▶ Stykkishólmur, on the peninsula's northern coast, is the region's largest town and a good base for overnighting.

▶ Even the well-trained and -outfitted are not allowed to ascend the glacier without a local guide; contact the National Park Visitor Centre in Malarrif, or take a tour.

✕ Take a Break

Hellnar has the small, welcoming **Primus Café** (☎865 6740; mains kr1500-2500; ☷10am-9pm May–mid-Sep, 11am-4pm mid-Sep–Apr) for simple meals. Fjöruhúsið (p120), by the rocky waterfront, serves soups and coffees with a wonderful view over seabird nests and the shore.

For reviews see

◉ Top Experiences	p108
◉ Experiences	p113
✕ Eating	p118
▣ Shopping	p122

0   10 km
0   5 miles

Flatey (18km);
Brjánslækur (30km)

Breiðafjörður

3 ❸ Breiðafjörður
5 ❺ Norska Húsið
11 ⓫ Volcano Museum

Helgafell (73m)
Skjöldur

Búðardalur (50km)

54
Drápuhlíðarfjall (527m)

Kerlingarfjall (585m)

Ljósufjöll

Harfursfell (722m)

Borgarnes (65km);
Reykjavík (137km)

Stykkishólmur

Vatnaleið

56
Kerlingarskarð

Miðhraun

Bjarnarhöfn 9 ◎
Shark Museum

Berserkjahraun

Hraunsfjarðarvatn

Setvallavatn

Þorgeirsfell

Baulárvallavatn

Hólsfjall

Vegamót

54
Stakkhamar

Hafffjörður

54
Grundarfjörður

✕13

Snæfellsnes
Peninsula

Lýsuhólslaug

Ytri-Tunga

Faxaflói

Kirkjufell 2 ◎

Helgrindur (986m)

Búlandshöfði

54
Fróðárheiði

Mælifell

Búðir

Church

Búðahraun

Búðir

Þúfubjarg

Búðaklettur

Breiðavík

Rif

16 ✕

Ingjaldshóll
Búrfell

574
Ólafsvík

19 ✕

Snæfellsjökull (1446m)

Rauðfeldsgjá

Sönghellir

Arnarstapi

17 ✕

Hellnar

Hellissandur

Skarðsvík
Rauðhólar

Eysteinsdalur

Klukkufoss

Neshraun

Snæfellsjökull
National Park ◉

Stapafell (526m)

Öndverðarnes

Svörtuloft
Fálki

Saxhólsbjarg
(bird cliffs)

574

Dritvík

Djúpalónssandur

Vatnshellir

Denmark
Strait

Breiðafjörður

Kirkjufell (p115)

Experiences

Langjökull

GLACIER

1 ⊙ Map p114, E4

The Langjökull ice cap is the second-largest glacier in Iceland, and the closest major glacier to Reykjavík. It's accessed from the Kaldidalur or Kjölur tracks, and its closest access village in West Iceland is Húsafell. Do not attempt to drive up onto the glacier yourself. Tours depart from Reykjavík or Húsafell: the Into the Glacier ice cave is a major tourist attraction, Mountaineers of Iceland (p135) offers snowmobiling, and **Dog Sledding** (☑863 6733; www.dogsledding.

is; tours from kr17,900) has summertime dog-sledding tours.

Into the Glacier

ICE CAVE

This enormous (300m-long) human-made tunnel and series of caves head into Langjökull glacier (see 1 ⊙ Map 114, E4) at 1260m above sea level. The glistening, LED-lit tunnel and caves opened in 2015 and contain exhibitions, a cafe and even a small chapel for those who want to tie the knot inside a glacier. Tours can be had from Húsafell or the glacier edge (adult/child kr19,500/free), from Reykjavík (kr29,900), or on many combo tours, such as snowmobiling, by helicopter, or including the Golden Circle.

20 km
10 miles

(Langjökull Ice Cave; ☎578 2550; www. intotheglacier.is; ⊙Mar-Oct)

Kirkjufell   MOUNTAIN

2 ◉ Map p112, C2

Kirkjufell (463m), guardian of Grundarfjörður's northwestern vista, is said to be one of the most photographed spots in Iceland. You'll see Ben Stiller skateboarding past in *The Secret Life of Walter Mitty* (2013). Ask the **Saga Centre** (Eyrbyggja Heritage Centre; ☎438 1881; www.grundarfjordur.is; Grundargata 35; ⊙9am-5pm) if you want to climb it, they may be able to get you a guide. Two spots involving a rope climb make it dangerous to scale when wet or without local knowledge. Kirkjufell is backed by the roaring waterfalls, **Kirkjufellsfoss**; more camera fodder.

Breiðafjörður   FJORD

3 ◉ Map p112, E1

Stykkishólmur's jagged peninsula pushes north into stunning Breiðafjörður, a broad waterway separating the Snæfellsnes from the looming cliffs of the distant Westfjords. According to local legend, there are only two things in the world that cannot be counted: the stars in the night sky and the craggy islets in the bay. You *can* count on epic vistas and a menagerie of wild birds (puffins, eagles, guillemots etc). Boat trips, including whale watching and puffin viewing, are available from Stykkishólmur, Grundarfjörður or Ólafsvík.

Viðgelmir – the Cave   LAVA TUBE

4 ◉ Map p114, D3

The easiest lava tube to visit, and the largest in Iceland, 1100-year-old, 1.5km-long Viðgelmir is located on private property near the farmstead Fljótstunga. It sparkles with ever-changing rock formations and has a stable walkway within it on which tours are conducted. Check the website for tour

Top Tip

Tours

▶ **Láki Tours** (☎546 6808; www.laki tours.com; Nesvegur 5) Puffins, whales and fishing from Grundarfjörður or Ólafsvík.

▶ **Seatours** (Sæferðir; ☎433 2254; www.seatours.is; Smiðjustígur 3; ⊙8am-8pm mid-May–mid-Sep, 9am-5pm mid-Sep–mid-May) Boat tours, including much-touted 'Viking Sushi', around Breiðafjörður.

▶ **Go West!** (☎695 9995; www.gowest. is) Biking, hiking and glacier tours.

▶ **Snæfellsjökull Glacier Tours** (☎663 3371; www.theglacier.is; snowcat/ snowmobile tours kr11,500/27,000; ⊙Mar-Jul) Snowcat and snowmobiles on Snæfellsjökull.

▶ **Lýsuhóll** (☎435 6716; www.lysuholl. is) and **Stóri Kambur** (☎852 7028; www.storikambur.is; ⊙Jun–mid-Sep) Horse riding in southern Snæfellsnes.

times; helmet and torch included.
(📞783 3600; www.thecave.is; tour per adult/
child from kr6500/free)

Norska Húsið
MUSEUM

5 Map p112, E1

Stykkishólmur's quaint maritime
charm comes from the cluster of
wooden warehouses, shops and
homes orbiting the town's harbour.
Most date back about 150 years. One
of the most interesting (and oldest) is
the Norska Húsið, now the regional
museum. Built by trader and amateur
astronomer Árni Thorlacius in 1832,
the house has been skilfully restored
and displays a wonderfully eclectic
selection of local antiquities. On the
2nd floor you can visit Árni's home,
an upper-class 19th-century residence, decked out with his original

wares. (Norwegian House; 📞433 8114;
www.norskahusid.is; Hafnargata 5, Stykkishólmur; adult/child kr800/free; ⏱11am-6pm
Jun-Aug, 2-5pm Tue-Thu Sep-May)

Krauma
HOT SPRINGS

6 Map p114, C3

Find Europe's biggest hot spring,
Deildartunguhver, about 5km west
of Reykholt, just off Rte 50, near the
junction with Rte 518. Look for billow-
ing clouds of steam, which rise from
scalding water bubbling from the
ground (180L per second and 100°C!).
A brand-new bathing complex called
Krauma opened in late 2016 and
offers sleek hot pools, a cold pool,
and two steam rooms. The scalding
spring water is mixed with cold water
from nearby Rauðsgil ravine, and
no chemicals are added. There's also

Understand
Egil's Saga

- -

Icelanders hold West Iceland in high regard for its canon of local sagas. The
famous *Egil's Saga* starts with the tale of Kveldúlfur, grandfather of warrior-
poet Egil Skallagrímsson (sometimes spelt Egill), who fled to Iceland during
the 9th century after a falling out with Norway's king. Kveldúlfur grew ill on
the journey, and instructed his son, Skallagrímur Kveldúlfsson, to throw his
coffin overboard after he died and build the family farm wherever it washed
ashore – this happened to be at Borg á Mýrum. Egil Skallagrímsson grew
up to be a fierce and creative individual who killed his first adversary at the
age of seven, went on to carry out numerous raids on Ireland, England and
Denmark, and saved his skin many a time by composing eloquent poetry.
Learn about him at Borgarnes' Settlement Centre (p108).

It is thought that one of the most important medieval chieftains and schol-
ars, Snorri Sturluson (1179–1241), may have written *Egil's Saga*. The Snorrastofa museum (p117) explores his legacy in sleepy inland hamlet Reykholt.

a restaurant. (Deildartunguhver; ☎555 6066; www.krauma.is; Rte 50; adult/child kr4900/2900; ◷10am-10pm)

Hraunfossar
WATERFALL

 7 Map p114, D3

The name of this spectacular waterfall translates to Lava Field Waterfall because the crystalline water streams out from below the lava field all around. Find the turn-out on the north side of Rte 518, 6.5km west of Húsafell. (Rte 518)

Snorrastofa
MUSEUM

 8 Map p114, C3

The interesting medieval study centre Snorrastofa is devoted to celebrated medieval poet, historian and statesman Snorri Sturluson, and is built on his old farm, where he was brutally slain. The centre contains displays explaining Snorri's life and accomplishments, including a 1599 edition of his *Heimskringla (Sagas of the Norse kings)*. There's material on the laws, literature and society of medieval Iceland, and on the excavations of the site. You can ask to see the modern church and reading room upstairs. (☎433 8000; www.snorrastofa.is; Reykholt; kr1200; ◷10am-6pm May-Aug, to 5pm Mon-Fri Sep-Apr)

Bjarnarhöfn Shark Museum
MUSEUM

 9 Map p112, D2

The farmstead at Bjarnarhöfn is the region's leading producer of *hákarl*

(fermented shark meat), a traditional Icelandic dish. The museum has exhibits on the history of this culinary curiosity, along with the family's fishing boats and processing tools. A video explains the butchering and fermenting procedure. Find the museum off Rte 54 on a turnout from Rte 577, on the fjord-side, northeastern edge of **Bjarnarhafnarfjall** (575m). (☎438 1581; www.bjarnarhofn.is; Bjarnarhöfn farm; adult/child kr1100/free; ◷9am-6pm Jun-Aug, reduced hours Sep-May)

Borgarfjördur Museum
MUSEUM

10 Map p114, B4

This small municipal museum has an engaging exhibit on the story of children in Iceland over the last

100 years. It's told through myriad photographs and found items, and though it's accompanied by English translations, don't be shy about having museum staff show you through. The story behind each photograph is captivating; you'll be thinking about this exhibit long after you've left. (Safnahús; ☑ 433 7200; www.safnahus. is; Bjarnarbraut 4-6, Borgarnes; adult/child kr1000/free; ⊙1-5pm May-Aug, 1-4pm Mon-Fri Sep-Apr)

Volcano Museum
MUSEUM

☑ 11 ◉ Map p112, E1

The Volcano Museum, housed in the town's old cinema, is the brainchild of vulcanologist Haraldur Sigurðsson, and features art depicting volcanoes, plus a small collection of

interesting lava ('magma bombs'!) and artefacts from eruptions. A film screens upstairs. (Eldfjallasafn; ☑ 433 8154; www.eldfjallasafn.is; Aðalgata 8, Stykkishólmur; adult/child kr1000/free; ⊙11am-5pm)

Hafnarfjall
MOUNTAIN

☑ 12 ◉ Map p114, B4

The dramatically sheer mountain Hafnarfjall (844m) rises south across the fjord from Borgarnes. You can climb it (7km) from the trailhead on Rte 1, near the southern base of the causeway into Borgarnes. Be careful of slippery scree cliffs once you ascend. You'll get sweeping views from the top.

Eating

Bjargarsteinn Mathús
SEAFOOD $$

☑ 13 ◉ Map p112, C2

This new restaurant on the point in Grundarfjörður is operated by seasoned restaurateurs who have created a lively menu of Icelandic dishes, with an emphasis on seafood and everything fresh. Desserts are delicious, and pretty, too. The seasonal menu is always changing, and views to Kirkjufell are stupendous. (☑ 438 6770; www.facebook.com/Bjargarsteinn restaurant; Sólvellir 15, Grundarfjörður; mains kr2900-4000; ⊙2-10pm Jun-Aug, 5-8pm Sep-May, closed mid-Dec–mid-Jan; ☎)

Local Life
A Climb & A Soak

A favourite Snæfellsnes hike is up roadside scoria crater **Saxhóll**, which was responsible for some of the lava on the western side of the peninsula. From the base it's a 300m climb for magnificent views over the Neshraun lava flows. Then head east over to **Lýsuhólslaug** (Map p112, C3; ☑433 9917; adult/child kr1000/3000; ⊙1.30-8.30pm Mon-Sat, to 6pm Sun Jul-Aug), where a geothermal source pumps in carbonated, mineral-filled waters at a perfect 37°C to 39°C. Don't be alarmed that the pool is a murky green: the iron-rich water attracts some serious algae.

Stykkishólmur harbour (p122)

Hótel Húsafell Restaurant

HOTEL $$$

14 Map p114, D3

The outstanding restaurant in this chic and contemporary new hotel serves creative, Icelandic cuisine showcasing superb ingredients and refined presentation. Art is the original work of local artist Páll Guðmundsson. (☑435 1551; www.hotelhusafell.com; Húsafell; mains lunch kr2000-4000, dinner kr4500-7000; P ☎)

Narfeyrarstofa

ICELANDIC $$

This charming restaurant in Stykkishólmur (see 3 ◉ Map 112, E1) is the Snæfellsnes' darling fine-dining destination. Book a table on the 2nd floor for the romantic lighting of antique lamps and harbour views. Ask your waiter about the portraits on the wall – the building has an interesting history. (☑438 1119; www.narfeyrarstofa.is; Aðalgata 3, Stykkishólmur; mains kr2000-5000; ◉11.30am-midnight Mon-Thu, to 1am Fri-Sun May-Sep, reduced hours Oct-Apr; ☑)

Settlement Centre Restaurant

INTERNATIONAL $$

15 Map p114, B4

The Settlement Centre's restaurant, in a light-filled room built into the rock face, is airy, upbeat, and one of the region's best bets for food. Choose from traditional Icelandic and international eats (lamb, fish stew etc). The lunch buffet (noon to 3pm) is very popular.

BANET / SHUTTERSTOCK ©

Q Local Life
Farm Food

Want to eat your way across the countryside? Make a beeline to **Erpsstaðir** (Map p114, B1; ✆868 0357; www.erpsstadir.is; Rte 60; cowshed adult/child kr650/free; ⏲1-5pm Jun–mid-Sep; ☷). Like a mirage for sweet-toothed wanderers, this dairy farm on the gorgeous Rte 60 (between Búðardalur and the Ring Road; with high mountain valleys, streams and waterfalls) specialises in delicious homemade ice cream (kr400). You can tour the farm, greet the buxom bovines, chickens, rabbits and even guinea pigs, then gorge on a scoop. Want more guidance? Join a **Crisscross Food Tour** (✆897 6140; www.crisscross. is) across West Iceland, with farm stops, snacks and a meal (full day kr39,500) while taking in local natural sites, from waterfalls to lava fields.

Book ahead for dinner. (✆437 1600; www.landnam.is; Brákarbraut 13, Borgarnes; lunch buffet kr2200, mains kr2200-5000; ⏲10am-9pm; ☷)

Gamla Rif
CAFE $

16 Map p112, B2

Gamla Rif is run by two fishermen's wives who have perfected a variety of traditional snacks. They dispense local travel tips with a smile, and serve tasty coffee and cakes. The show-stopper is their fish soup (from their husbands' daily catch) with fresh bread; don't miss it. (✆436 1001; Háarif 3, Rif; cakes from kr850, fish soup kr1900; ⏲noon-8pm Jun-Aug; ☷)

Fjöruhúsið
SEAFOOD $$

17 Map p112, B3

It's well worth following the stone path down to the ocean's edge for the renowned fish soup at beautifully situated, quaint Fjöruhúsið in Hellnar. Located by the bird cliffs at the trailhead of the scenic Hellnar–Arnarstapi path, it also serves coffee in sweet, old-fashioned china. (✆435 6844; Hellnar; cake & quiche kr950, mains kr2500-2800; ⏲11am-10pm Jun-Aug, reduced hours Mar-May & Sep-Nov)

Sjávarpakkhúsið
ICELANDIC $$

This old fish-packing house in Stykkishólmur (see 3 Map 112, E1) has been transformed into a wood-lined cafe-bar with harbour-front outdoor seating. The speciality is blue-shell mussels straight from the bay, but it's also a great daytime hang-out. On weekend evenings it turns into a popular bar where locals come to jam. (✆438 1800; Hafnargata 2, Stykkishólmur; mains kr2600-3500; ⏲noon-11pm Sun-Thu, to 3am Fri & Sat Jun-Aug, reduced hours Sep-May; ☷)

Plássið
ICELANDIC $$

Located in in Stykkishólmur (see 3 Map 112, E1), this bistro-style old-town building is a perfect family-friendly spot, with elegant touches (wine glasses, mod furnishings) and friendly service. Using local ingredients,

Countryside near Hellnar

it serves up a full run of regional specials, and the catch of the day is usually delicious, paired with salad or barley risotto. Local beers, too. New management took over in late 2016; we'll see if they can keep it going! (📞436 1600; www.plassid.is; Frúarstígur 1, Stykkishólmur; mains kr2500-5000; ⏲11.30am-10pm May-Sep; 🏃👪)

Englendingavík   CAFE $$

Casual and friendly, with a wonderful waterfront deck, Englendingavík serves good homemade dishes, from cakes to full meals of roast lamb or fresh fish. It has an attached guesthouse (doubles with shared bathroom from kr14,600) in a recently restored building. It's located in Borgarnes (see 15 🍴 Map 114, B4). (📞555 1400; www.englendingavik.is; Skúlgata 17, Borgarnes; mains kr2450-4500; ⏲11.30am-11pm May-Sep, reduced hours Oct-Apr; 🛜🏃)

Ok Bistro   ICELANDIC $$

18 🍴 Map p114, B4

Make your way to the 3rd floor in a modern business building to this refined dining room with sweeping fjord and mountain views. The emphasis here is on locally sourced ingredients creatively prepared. Order tapas style and share or go for beautifully presented large mains. In case you're wondering, the restaurant is named after the 1200m mountain

named Ok. (📞437 1200; www.okbistro.
is; Digranesgata 2, Borgarnes; small courses
kr2000-3000, large courses kr3700-5000;
🕐11.30am-10pm; 🛜)

Fosshotel Hellnar Restaurant
ICELANDIC **$$**

Even if you're not overnighting at
Hótel Hellnar, we highly recommend
having dinner at its restaurant (see
17 ❌ Map 112, B3), which sources local
organic produce for its Icelandic
menu, plus offers heavenly *skyr* cake
for dessert. Reserve ahead. (📞435
6820; Hellnar; dinner mains kr3500-5600;
🕐6-9.30pm Mar-Oct; 🅿🛜)

Hraun
INTERNATIONAL **$$**

19 Map p112, B2

This upbeat establishment on the
main road cheerfully fills a blond-

Local Life
Stykkishólmur

The charming town of Stykkishólmur (Map 112, E1), the largest on
the Snæfellsnes Peninsula, is built
around a natural harbour tipped
by a basalt islet. It's a picturesque
place with a laid-back attitude and
a sprinkling of brightly coloured
buildings from the late 19th century, featured in Ben Stiller's *The
Secret Life of Walter Mitty* (2013).
With a comparatively good choice
of accommodation and restaurants,
and transport links, Stykkishólmur
makes an excellent base for exploring the region.

wood building with a broad front
deck. The only gig in town besides fast
food, it does excellent fresh mussels,
burgers and fish, and has beer on tap.
(📞431 1030; Grundarbraut 2, Ólafsvík; mains
kr2000-5000; 🕐noon-10pm Jun-Aug, some
weekends Sep-May; 🛜)

Drinking

Steðji Brugghús
BREWERY

20 🍺 Map p114, C4

This little family-run brewhouse 25km
north of Borgarnes off Rte 50 has a
good range of local beers, from straw-
berry beer to lager and seasonal beers.
Try them all in its brand-new tasting
room. (📞896 5001; www.stedji.com; tasting
kr1500; 🕐1-5pm Mon-Sat)

Entertainment

Freezer Hostel
THEATRE, LIVE MUSIC

Check online for the program at this
cool theatre and live-music venue
housed in a hostel in Rif (see **16** ❌ Map
112, B2). In summer there's an active
program of plays, storytelling and
music. (📞865 9432; www.thefreezer
hostel.com; Hafnargata 16; dm/apt from
kr6100/28,500; 🛜)

Shopping

Ljómalind
MARKET

A recent collaboration between local producers, this packed farmers

ANNAPURNA MELLOR / GETTY IMAGES ©

Traditional Icelandic wool jumpers

market sits at the edge of Borgarnes (see 15 ⊗ Map 114, B4), near the roundabout. It stocks everything from fresh dairy from Erpsstaðir (p120) and organic meat, to locally made bath products, handmade wool sweaters, jewellery and all manner of imaginative collectables. (Farmers Market; ♪437 1400; www.ljomalind.is; Brúartorg 4, Borgarnes; ⊙10am-6pm May-Aug, reduced hours Sep-Apr)

Ullarselið CLOTHING, ARTS & CRAFTS

21 🔒 Map p114, B4

Find your way to off-the-beaten-path village Hvanneyri, 12km east of Borgarnes, and in among fjord-side homes you'll find this fantastic wool

centre. Handmade sweaters, scarves, hats and blankets share space with skeins of beautiful hand-spun yarn, and interesting bone and shell buttons. For beginners, there are needles and patterns to get you started. (♪437 0077; www.ull.is; Hvanneyri; ⊙11am-5pm Jun-Aug, 1-5pm Thu-Sat Sep-May)

Leir 7 ARTS & CRAFTS

Artist Sigríður Erla produces tableware from the fjord's dark clay at this pottery studio in the heart of Stykkishólmur (see 3 ⊙ Map 112, E1). There's also woodcraft. (www.leir7.is; Aðalgata 20, Stykkishólmur; ⊙2-5pm Mon-Fri, to 4pm Sat)

The Best of
Reykjavík

Reykjavík's Best Walks

Reykjavík's Best...

Reykjavík Roasters (p62)

Best Walks
Historic Reykjavík

🏃 The Walk

The earliest signs of settlement in Reykjavík date to just before 871 and are centred in the Old Reykjavík quarter. Norwegian Viking Ingólfur Arnarson is credited with being the country's first permanent inhabitant. He made his home in a promising-looking bay that he named Reykjavík (Smoky Bay), after the steam from its thermal springs. This walk takes in the highlights of Ingólfur's historic neighbourhood.

Start Kraum

Finish National Museum

Length 1.6km; 1½ hours

✕ Take a Break

Stop for a coffee on Austurvöllur square, or across the street at smart bistro Nora Magasin (p32), for a quick tipple or a more substantial meal.

LEONID ANDRONOV / SHUTTERSTOCK ©

Fríkirkjan í Reykjavík

❶ Historic House

Reykjavík's oldest timber house dates to 1762, and sits on Aðalstræti, one of the capital's oldest streets. The house is now home to **Cintamani** (p67), a well-known Icelandic outdoors-wear brand.

❷ The Settlement Exhibition

Beneath **The Settlement Exhibition** (p26) lies a 10th-century Viking longhouse, which was discovered by chance and excavated in 2001 when the hotel next door was renovated. Curators have recreated the dimly lit mood of the longhouse but have tricked it out with multimedia displays bringing the era to life.

❸ Skúli Magnússon Statue

Across from The Settlement Exhibition, there's a **statue** of powerful town magistrate-sheriff Skúli Magnússon (1711–94), who organised the building of weaving, tanning and wool-dyeing factories in the capital –

the foundations of the modern city of Reykjavík.

❹ Austurvöllur

Once part of settler Ingólfur Arnarson's meadows, **Austurvöllur** (p30) sits next to the **Alþingi** (parliament; p30) and in its centre there's a statue of Jón Sigurðsson (1811–79), who led the campaign for Icelandic independence. The adjacent cathedral, **Dómkirkja** (p32), was built in the 18th century.

❺ Iðnó

As you approach lake Tjörnin, you'll see the waterside **Ráðhús** (city hall; p30). Inside there's a fun topographical map of Iceland. **Iðnó** (Iðnaðarmannahúsið; The Craftsmen's House) was designed and built by Einar Pálsson in 1896 and was the city's main meeting hall, and for many years a theatre.

❻ Around Tjörnin

As you make your way around the banks of **Tjörnin** (p29), which is called 'The Pond'

by locals, you'll pass the quaint church, **Fríkirkjan í Reykjavík**, the **National Gallery of Iceland** (p56) and **Hljómskálagarður Park** (p29), which contains sculptures by five historic Icelandic artists.

❼ National Museum

The **National Museum** (p24) traces human history in Iceland, from the earliest settlement to the modern era. There are also rotating photographic exhibits and a welcoming cafe.

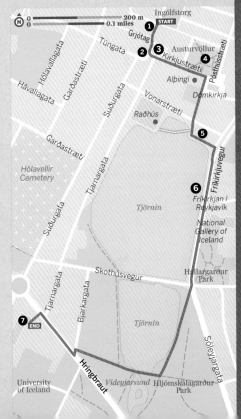

Best Walks
Reykjavík Art & Design

🏃 The Walk

Icelanders have a knack for piquant, arresting art and design. The city is littered with local creations, including modernist architecture, cool contemporary art, and shops full of functional but creative crafts and design gadgets. This walk takes you through a sampling of the disciplines, all in a compact, popular section of central Reykjavík.

Start Reykjavík Art Museum – Kjarvalsstaðir

Finish Harpa concert hall

Length 3km; two hours

🍴 Take a Break

Stop for a delicious, organic meal at Gló (p58), where the menu changes daily and is accompanied by a broad bar of intricate and flavourful salads. A colourful crew of locals crowds in for popular lunches, and plenty of bars and coffee shops sit just nearby.

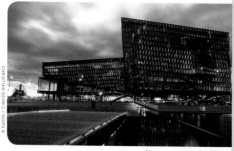

CHRISTIAN GEHRIG / 500PX ©

Harpa concert hall (p55)

❶ Reykjavík Art Museum – Kjarvalsstaðir

The **Kjarvalsstaðir** (p56) looks onto Miklatún Park, and is named for Jóhannes Kjarval (1885–1972), one of Iceland's most popular classical artists. The peaceful museum displays his wonderfully evocative landscapes and also the works of many major 20th-century Icelandic painters.

❷ Einar Jónsson Museum

Einar Jónsson (1874–1954) was one of Iceland's foremost sculptors, with his dramatic allegorical style. The **Einar Jónsson Museum** (p57) fills the studio he designed. Upper stories have city views; the **sculpture garden** (p57) behind it is free.

❸ Hallgrímskirkja

Guðjón Samúelsson (1887–1950), perhaps Iceland's most renowned 20th-century architect, created a distinctive Icelandic aesthetic. Reykjavík's

Hallgrímskirkja (p50) is perhaps the pinnacle of his work. Pop around the corner to classic 1937 swimming pool **Sundhöllin** (p57), to see another example.

④ Design Shops

Icelandic artists and designers create many objects that combine beauty and practicality. Laugavegur is loaded with shops selling designers' work. To the east, **Kiosk** (p65) is a couture cooperative. **KronKron** (p66) has top clothes, but its handmade shoes are off the charts. To the west, **Skúmaskot** (p65) is packed with unique handmade art and clothing.

⑤ Art

Walk to the ocean's edge for the popular *Sun Voyager (Sólfar)* sculpture. *Sun Voyager* was created by Jón Gunnar Árnason, and its skeletal shiplike frame sits powerfully along the water, with snow-topped mountains in the distance.

⑥ Harpa Concert Hall

Reykjavík's dazzling **Harpa concert hall** (p55), with its facade of glimmering hexagons, opened in 2011 and was designed by Danish firm Henning Larsen Architects, Icelandic firm Batteríið Architects, and Danish-Icelandic artist Olafur Eliasson. Be sure to zip inside to see its vaulted glass panels and wonderful harbour sightlines.

Best
Eating

Yes, Icelanders love hot dogs, and there are boundary-pushing dishes such as fermented shark or sheep's head. But the spotlight shines brightest on Iceland's fresh-from-the-farm ingredients, seafood hauled from its icy waters, innovative dairy products (hello, *skyr*!) or the historic food-preserving techniques that are finding new favour with today's New Nordic chefs.

NEIL JOHN SMITH / GETTY IMAGES ©

Food Culture

Reykjavík is not only the political but the culinary capital of Iceland. Choose from a vibrant cafe-bar scene, where effortlessly cool Reykjavikers hang out sipping fine coffees and munching cakes, waffles or tapas, or top-of-the-heap Icelandic restaurants, that take local cuisine to its most rarefied extremes.

Icelandic Specialities

If you see a queue in Reykjavík, it probably ends at a *pylsur* (hot dog) stand. *Fiskisúpa* (fish soup) comes courtesy of family recipes, while *kjötsúpa* (meat soup) usually features veggies and chunks of lamb. Icelandic lamb is hard to beat, with free-range sheep munching chemical-free grasses and herbs.

In the past, Icelanders merely kept the cheeks and tongues of *þorskur* (cod) – a delicacy – and exported the rest; but today you'll commonly find cod fillets on the menu, along with *ýsa* (haddock) and *bleikja* (Arctic char). During the summer find *silungur* (freshwater trout) and *villtur lax* (wild salmon).

You'll also see wild animals such whale, *hákarl* (fermented shark) and *lundi* (puffin; although there has been worrying crash in puffin numbers).

Don't miss *skyr*, a yoghurt-like concoction made from pasteurised skimmed milk.

☑ **Top Tips**

▶ Reserve ahead in summer for top restaurants.

▶ Even in summer, restaurants may stop serving around 9pm.

▶ Be aware that there are significant conservation issues with whale, puffin and shark.

Best Food on the Go

Bæjarins Beztu
Reykjavík's legendary hot-dog stand. (p32)

Lobster Hut Get your lobster on the go...as a sandwich or salad. (p34)

Fish & Chips Tiny food truck at the Old Harbour with delectable, yes, fish and chips. (p44)

Grillmarkaðurinn (p32)

Hamborgara Búllan Reykjavík's favourite burgers. (p44)

Best Fine Dining

Dill Arguably one of Reykjavík's finest restaurants, with elaborate tasting menus. (p58)

Matur og Drykkur Top, refined Icelandic cuisine; book ahead to get in. (p43)

Apotek Cool, interesting new restaurant perfect for sharing small plates and cocktails. (p32)

Grillmarkaðurinn Formal, fancy and fantastic meals presented with attention to detail. (p32)

Messinn Piping hot skillets of fresh fish served with aplomb. (p32)

Þrír Frakkar Top Icelandic dishes in a cosy dining room. (p59)

Best Restaurants Outside Reykjavík

Bjargarsteinn Mathús In Grundarfjörður, run by an award-winning chef. (p118)

Slippurinn In Heimaey, with a lively vibe, overlooking the harbour. (p102)

Narfeyrarstofa Reliably delicious and romantic in Stykkishólmur. (p119)

Lindin Lakeside in Laugarvatn, with fantastic wild-caught mains. (p88)

Best Local

Bakarí Sandholt Some of the capital's best

baked goods, sandwiches and sweets. (p60)

Grái Kötturinn Tiny and great for breakfasts and brunch. (p59)

Hverfisgata 12 No sign, but pizza and cocktails. What more could you want? (p61)

Við Fjöruborðið Oceanside seafood in Stokkseyri with yummy lobster bisque. (p96)

Vitabar Scrumptious burgers in a Reykjavík bar. (p61)

Best Veg-Organic

Gló Fresh, organic and loaded with tasty herbs and spices. (p58)

Garðurinn Organic and vegan specialities change daily. (p61)

Best
Cafes & Bars

The city's ratio of coffee houses and bars to citizens is impressive. Handcrafted coffees and designer microbrews are prepared with zeal for accidental hipsters sporting *lopapeysur* (Icelandic woollen sweaters). In fact, the local social scene is built around low-key cafes that crank up the intensity after hours, when tea is swapped for tipples and dance moves break out.

TRAVELSTOCK44 / LOOK-FOTO / GETTY IMAGES ©

Best Cafes

Reykjavík Roasters Coffee aficionados roast their own beans; now with two branches. (p62)

Kaffi Vínyl Sip coffee or cocktails while listening to laid-back tunes. (p62)

Stofan Kaffihús Spacious and welcoming in a historic Old Reykjavík building. (p33)

Kaffi Mokka One of the capital's oldest cafes with an approachable, well-worn feel. (p62)

Café Haiti In the Old Harbour, with coffee sourced from Haiti. (p47)

C is for Cookie Tiny and in a relaxed residential side street. (p63)

Best Cocktail Bars

Slippbarinn Cocktails and tunes abound at this harbourfront bar-restaurant. (p47)

Apotek Glittering glass and bubbly conversation pairs perfectly with top-flight cocktails. (p32)

Loftið High-end cocktail bars with a jazzy feel. (p35)

Best Local

Kaffibarinn A Reykjavík institution, which is chilled by day and packed on weekend nights. (p53)

Kaldi Effortlessly cool with its own microbrews on tap. (p52)

Prikið A quintessential dive bar with good stick to-your-ribs diner food. (p53)

Boston The arty crowd hangs out here; it's above Laugavegur. (p53)

Dillon Rock bar with frequent live music. (p53)

Best Streetside People-Watching

Bravó Local beer on tap and good happy hours on a busy Laugavegur corner. (p62)

Café Paris On the edge of Old Reykjavík's Austurvöllur square; grab a drink and watch the action. (p27)

Best Late-Night

Paloma Two DJ spaces and an ever-changing line-up. (p35)

Húrra Early happy hour and late-night DJs or live music. (p36)

Kiki Dance the night away in this multistorey club. (p53)

Best
Museums, Exhibitions & Galleries

ÁSMUNDUR SVEINSSON ARTWORK AT THE REYKJAVIK ART MUSEUM

EDUCATION IMAGES / GETTY IMAGES ©

Best Art Museums

Reykjavík Art Museum Three wonderful branches included in one ticket: large, downtown Hafnarhús (p29) focusing on contemporary art; Kjarvalsstaðir (p56), with 20th-century art; and Ásmundarsafn (pictured right; p69) for sculptures by Ásmundur Sveinsson.

National Gallery of Iceland Constantly changing lakeside collection of Iceland's finest artists. (p56)

Reykjavík Museum of Photography Annual exhibitions of primarily Scandinavian photography. (p30)

Sigurjón Ólafsson Museum Oceanside sculpture with sea breezes, totem poles and busts. (p69)

Best History Museums

National Museum All of Iceland's best artefacts gathered under one well-curated roof. (p24)

The Settlement Exhibition Excellent multimedia exhibits and an excavated Viking longhouse. (p26)

Settlement Centre Borgarnes' interesting examination of Settlement times and the well-known *Egil's Saga*. (p108)

Culture House An excellently curated combination of art and artefacts tracing Iceland's history. (p55)

Sögusetrið Hvolsvöllur's museum dedicated to the local *Njál's Saga*. (p100)

Best Off-Beat Museums & Exhibitions

Icelandic Phallological Museum Fascinating, yes fascinating, array of Icelandic penises – all of the mammals are represented. (p56)

Draugasetrið Goulish haunted house in Stokkseyri, with spooky tales and dried ice. (p96)

Saga Museum Silicon models and dioramas bringing the gory, thrilling hijinks of Settlement to life. (p41)

Best Natural Phenomena

Volcano House Watch movies of Icelandic volcanoes erupting. (p30)

Aurora Reykjavík Learn about and watch a simulation of the Northern Lights. (p43)

Best Art Galleries

i8 Famous Icelandic and international contemporary artists. (p30)

Kling & Bang Young, up-and-comers in the art world. (p42)

Nýló Contemporary art and performances. (p43)

Best
Tours

Reykjavík makes a superb base for loads of regional tours to the wild outdoors. Whether you're simply not up for renting your own wheels, or you want to head to areas that require expert guidance or serious equipment, you'll find a tour to suit almost any time frame, need or skill level. Many regional operators also pick up from Reykjavík.

BAHADIR YENICERI / SHUTTERSTOCK ©

Reykjavík Tours

The tourist office has free maps and self-guided walking tour brochures, and info on guided walking tours. The hardcore can buy the more in-depth *Reykjavík Walks* (Guðjón Friðriksson; 2014) at local bookshops. There are several smartphone apps, including those by Locatify (Smartguide) and Reykjavík Sightseeing.

☑ **Top Tips**

▶ Companies offer all sorts of tours in myriad combinations. Check online with each company for its full menu.

Best Reykjavík Tours

Literary Reykjavík (www. bokmenntaborgin.is; Tryggvagata 15; admission free; ◷3pm Thu Jun-Aug) Walking tours of the centre start at the main library. A *Literary Reykjavík* app is also available.

Free Walking Tour Reykjavik (www.freewalkingtour.is; admission free; ◷noon & 2pm Jun-Aug, reduced hours winter) One-hour, 1.5km walking tour of the centre.

City Sightseeing Reykjavík (☎580 5400; www. city-sightseeing.com; adult/child kr3500/free; ◷half-hourly 9.30am-4.30pm mid-May–mid-Sep) Hop-on, hop-off bus taking in major sights around town.

Best Bicycle Tours

Reykjavík Bike Tours & Segway Tours (☎694 8956; www.icelandbike.com; Ægisgarður 7, Old Harbour; bike rental per 4hr from kr3500, tours from kr6500; ◷9am-5pm Jun-Aug, re-

duced hours Sep-May; 🚌14) Bike hire and tours of Reykjavík and surrounds.

Bike Company (☎590 8550; http://bikecompany. is; Faxafen 8) Bicycle tours throughout the region.

Best Bus Tours

Reykjavík Excursions (Kynnisferðir; ☎580 5400; www.re.is; BSÍ Bus Terminal, Vatnsmýrarvegur 10) Popular bus operator. Summer and winter programs.

Iceland Excursions (Gray Line Iceland; ☎540 1313; www.grayline.is; Hafnar-

Horse riding near Landmannalaugar (p100)

stræti 20) Large groups on comprehensive day trips.

Sterna (☎551 1166; www.sterna.is; Harpa concert hall, Austurbakki 2; ☺7am–midnight Jun–Aug) More modest-sized operator.

Gateway to Iceland (☎534 4446; www.gtice.is) Small groups and good guides.

Go Green (☎694 9890, 551 9854; www.gogreen.is) High-end with sustainable practices.

Best Adventure Tours

Arctic Adventures (☎562 7000; www.adventures.is; Laugavegur 11; ☺8am–10pm) Young, enthusiastic action-filled tours.

Icelandic Mountain Guides (☎587 9999; www.mountainguides.is;

Stórhöfði 33) Specialists in mountaineering, ice climbing and the like.

Midgard Adventure (p98) One of South Iceland's best adventure operators.

Mountaineers of Iceland (☎580 9900; www.mountaineers.is) Excellent guides; lots of super-Jeep, super-truck and snowmobiling tours.

Inside the Volcano (☎863 6640; www.insidethevolcano.com; tours kr42,000; ☺mid-May–mid-Oct) Amazing trip into an intact 4000-year-old magma chamber.

Best Horse Riding Tours

Eldhestar (☎480 4800; www.eldhestar.is; Vellir, Hveragerði) Near Hveragerði,

rides on surrounding grasslands.

Íshestar (☎555 7000; www.ishestar.is; Sörlaskeið 26, Hafnarfjörður) One of the oldest stables with trots through lava fields.

Best Air Tours

Eagle Air (☎562 4200; www.eagleair.is; Reykjavík Domestic Airport) Sightseeing flights over volcanoes and glaciers.

Air Iceland (☎570 3030; www.airiceland.is; Reykjavík Domestic Airport) Combination air, bus, hiking, rafting, horse-riding, whale-watching and glacier tours around Iceland.

Atlantsflug (☎854 4105; www.flightseeing.is; Reykjavík Domestic Airport) Flightseeing tours from Reykjavík, Bakki Airport and Skaftafell.

Best
Natural Wonders

It is an absolute must to take a day trip or an overnight outside of Reykjavík to take in some of the incredible volcanic landscapes, geothermal fields, glaciers, dramatic fjords and black-sand seashores. In summer, bird life can be abundant, with puffins flapping and Arctic terns diving. And from October to April look for the Northern Lights.

Best Volcanoes

Hekla Once thought to be the gates of hell; you can climb it. (p99)

Eyjafjallajökull Stopped air traffic in Europe in 2010. (pictured right; p100)

Eldfell Small, but almost smothered Heimaey in lava in 1973. (p99)

Reykjanes Peninsula Four volcanic chains in action. (p74)

Best Glaciers

Vatnajökull The largest ice cap in Europe with glacier tongues and a giant park to match. (p103)

Langjökull Site of a tour-able ice cave in West Iceland. (p113)

Snæfellsjökull So awesome it has its own

national park in West Iceland. (p111)

Sólheimajökull Accessible from Mýrdalsjökull ice cap. (p97)

Best Waterfalls

Gullfoss The 'Golden Falls' course over rock tiers and down a gorge. (p82)

Seljalandsfoss Walk behind the curtain of this cascade. (p96)

Skógafoss Dreamy and huge; just to the west of Skógar. (p98)

Svartifoss Skaftafell's falls plummet from black basalt columns. (p103)

Best Lava Tubes

Víðgelmir Iceland's largest lava tube, accessible by guided tour; in West Iceland. (p115)

Vatnshellir Much-loved lava tube in West Iceland's Snæfellsjökull National Park. (p111)

Best Geothermal Springs

Blue Lagoon Vibrant turquoise and world-famous. (p73)

Gamla Laugin Refurbished historic spring in meadows. (p85)

Krauma New spa complex at Europe's biggest hot spring. (p116)

Fontana Chic and lakeside in Laugarvatn. (p85)

Lýsuhólslaug Bubbly water on the south coast of the Snæfellsnes Peninsula. (p118)

Laugardalslaug Reykjavík's historic springs, now a giant bathing complex. (p69)

Best **With Kids**

Best Parks

Reykjavík Zoo & Family Park What's not to love? Farm animals, floaty rafts, kids' ride, all in a grand park. (p69)

Tjörnin Get your crumbs and feed the ducks at the pretty lake. (p29)

Hljómskálagarður Examine interesting sculptures throughout the park. (p29)

Geothermal Park Boil an egg in the thermal vents in Hveragerði.(p86)

Best Sights

Hallgrímskirkja Take the elevator to the top of the church for thrilling views. (p50)

Volcano House Watch movies of exploding volcanoes. (p30)

Saga Museum See silicon representations of the Sagas, then dress up in costume for photos. (p41)

Whales of Iceland Look at amazing life-size replicas of all the Icelandic whales. (p42)

Omnom Chocolate Tour a local chocolate factory. (p42)

Aurora Reykjavík Try out the Northern Lights simulator. (p43)

Best Swims

Laugardalslaug Giant pool complex with water slide. (pictured right; p69)

Blue Lagoon Teal water and silica mud for horseplay. (p73)

Gamla Laugin Huge geothermal pool by a burbling stream. (p85)

Best Day Trips

Viðey Island Bike and hike on a windswept coastal island. (p70)

Geysir Watch the geyser shoot water wonderfully high. (p80)

River Rafting Strap 'em in for a zip down the Hvítá river. (p88)

MAGNUS HJORLEIFSSON/GETTY IMAGES ©

☑ Top Tips

▶ Children's admission to museums and swimming pools varies from 50% to free. They pay adult fees at anywhere from 12 to 18.

▶ Kids usually get 50% off with tour companies.

Horse Riding Take a trot on an Icelandic pony. (p97)

Best Food

Bæjarins Beztu Reykjavík's favourite hot dogs. (p32)

Valdi's Homemade ice cream and happy families. (p43)

Best
Shopping

Reykjavík's vibrant design culture and craft-oriented ethos makes for great shopping: from edgy fashion and knitted *lopapeysur* (Icelandic woollen sweaters) to unique music and loads of lip-smacking liquor. Many artists and designers form collectives and open shops and galleries, full of handmade, beautiful work: everything from striking bowls made out of radishes to fish-skin handbags, creative toys and cool couture.

ICELANDIC PHOTO AGENCY • ALAMY STOCK PHOTO ©

Design

The Iceland Design Centre (www.icelanddesign.is) promotes local designers' work, and you can check online for the latest news, exhibitions and events, as well as interesting blog posts. Its DesignMarch annual event opens hundreds of exhibitions and workshops to the public.

Sweaters & Knitting

Hand- or machine-made *lopapeysur* and other wool products are staples of Icelandic life, and of many souvenir shops. Individual regions have their own motifs. For example, Borgafjörður designs feature geese, ptarmigan or salmon. Handmade garments made from local wool don't come cheap. Prices in the countryside can be somewhat lower than Reykjavík tourist shops, and you'll know the true knitting stores because they also sell yarn, patterns and needles.

Icelandic Culture and Craft Workshops (p58) offer half-day knitting workshops using pure Icelandic wool. Designer Hélène Magnússon offers knitting tours (http://icelandicknitter.com) that take in spinning, wool work, design, folklore and hiking/sightseeing.

Best Fashion

Kiosk Local designers of women's clothing. (p65)

KronKron From international couture to Scandi designers, and handmade shoes. (pictured right; p66)

Jör Of-the-moment clothes and accessories by hot designer Guðmundur Jörundsson. (p67)

Steinunn Wildly creative knits feature in this couture collection. (p47)

Geysir One of the local favourites for inventive clothing. (p66)

66° North Premier outdoor clothes. (p67)

Best Design

Kirsuberjatréð A Reykjavík institution, with high-end excellent arts and crafts. (p37)

Kraum All manner of gadgets, gewgaws and garb. (pictured left; p64)

Skúmaskot Ten local designers making everything from pottery to kids' clothes. (p65)

Reykjavík's Cutest Small house packed with local design items. (p67)

Best Knitting & Traditional Knitwear

Handknitting Association of Iceland Two city centre shops full of knits; the Skólavörðustígur 19 location also has yarn, patterns and needles. (p66)

Álafoss Lots of local knits; plus outlet store in Mosfellsbær. (p66)

Ullarselið Countryside knitting in a tiny village,

12km east of Borgarnes. (p123)

Víkurprjón In Vík and open 24 hours; it also demonstrates knitting machines. (p103)

Best Souvenirs

Rammagerðin – Iceland Gift Store Multiple branches loaded with higher-end mementos, art and fashion. (p65)

Blue Lagoon Shop Algae masks for all your friends! (p67)

Best Music

Lucky Records Low-key and off the beaten path, but packed with rare grooves. (p64)

12 Tónar Famous, casual store fun for hanging out. (p64)

Best Local

Frú Lauga Farmers market with products from all over Iceland. (p69)

Kolaportið Flea Market Second-hand toys sit alongside fermented shark at this weekend market. (p37)

Ljómalind Borgarnes' farmers market with local eats, knitwear, crafts and more. (p122)

Mál og Menning Reykjavikers loiter over coffee and browse books in this multi-storey independent bookshop. (p66)

Best Liquor

Keflavík International Airport The airport's arrivals hall duty free shops. (p17)

Vínbúðin The national liquor store chain is the only game in town. (p46)

Best
Festivals

Icelanders celebrate festivals with gleeful enthusiasm. While Reykjavík is the epicentre of the excitement, even small villages have their own festivities: for local heroes, civic pride or just good, old-fashioned traditions. Almost everyone participates, and a spirit of good cheer usually applies. The Reykjavík festivals are also a super showcase for Icelandic and international music and art.

AGE FOTOSTOCK / ALAMY STOCK PHOTO ©

Best Music Festivals

Iceland Airwaves (www. icelandairwaves.is) Since the first edition of Iceland Airwaves in 1999, this fab November festival has become one of the world's premier annual showcases for new music (Icelandic and otherwise).

Þjóðhátíð (www.dal urinn.is) In Heimaey, Vestmannaeyjar, on the August long weekend, more than 11,000 people descend to watch bands and fireworks, and drink gallons of alcohol.

Secret Solstice (www. secretsolstice.is) This excellent festival coincides with the solstice, so there's 24-hour daylight too. Held at Laugardalur in Reykjavík.

Skálholt Summer Concerts (www.sumarton leikar.is) The cathedral at the historic religious centre of Skálholt hosts around 40 concerts, lectures and workshops from July to August.

Reykjavík Jazz Festival (www.reykjavikjazz. is) From mid-August, Reykjavík toe-taps its way through a week dedicated to jazz, man. Local and international musicians blow their own trumpets at Harpa.

Sónar Reykjavík (www. sonarreykjavik.com) Music, creativity and technology: this festival brings all three together for three days at Harpa concert hall, with over 70 bands and DJs from Iceland and abroad.

Dark Music Days (www. darkmusicdays.is) A mid-winter music festival at Harpa concert hall featuring Icelandic composers.

Best Arts Festivals

Reykjavík Arts Festival (www.listahatid. is) Culture vultures flock to Iceland's premier cultural festival in late May or early June for two weeks of local and international theatre, film, dance, music and visual art.

Reykjavík Culture Night (Menningarnótt; www. menningarnott.is) Mid-August, Reykjavíkers turn out for a day and night of art, music, dance and fireworks. Galleries, shops, cafes and churches stay open until late.

DesignMarch (www. designmarch.is) Local

Secret Solstice music festival

design is celebrated in Reykjavík at this four-day feast of all things aesthetically pleasing: from fashion to furniture, architecture to food design.

Reykjavík International Film Festival (www.riff. is) Intimate 11-day event from late September features quirky programming highlighting local and international independent film-making.

Reykjavík International Literary Festival (www. bokmenntahatid.is) This venerable festival gathers international writers for four days of readings and panels in September.

Best Cultural Festivals

National Day The country's biggest holiday commemorates the founding of the Republic of Iceland on 17 June 1944 with parades and general patriotic merriness.

Reykjavík Pride (www. hinsegindagar.is) Out and proud since 1999, this festival brings Carnival-like colour to the capital on the second weekend of August. About 90,000 people attended 2014's Pride march and celebrations.

Þorrablót This Viking midwinter feast (late January to mid-/late February) is marked nationwide with stomach-churning treats such as *hákarl* (fermented shark), *svið* (singed sheep's head) and *hrútspungar* (rams' testicles). All accompanied by shots of *brennivín* (a potent schnapps nicknamed 'black death').

Food & Fun (www. foodandfun.is) In March, international chefs team up with local restaurants and vie for awards at this capital feast.

Verslunarmannahelgi The first weekend in August is a public-holiday long weekend when Icelanders flock to rural festivals, family barbecues, rock concerts and wild campground parties.

Seafarers' Day (*Sjó-mannadagurinn*) Fishing is integral to Icelandic life, and Seafarers' Day is party time in fishing villages. On the first weekend in June, every ship in Iceland is in harbour and all sailors have a day off.

Best
For Free

Best Natural Wonders

Þingvellir Iceland's original parliament site, in a dramatic rift valley. (p78)

Geysir Watch the geothermal water spout like clockwork. (p80)

Gullfoss The famous Golden Falls tumble down a narrow canyon. (p82)

Reynisfjara Gorgeous black-sand beach near Vík with basalt columns, caves, puffins and sea stacks. (p96)

Dyrhólaey Photogenic rock arch off the coast of Vík, with seabird breeding grounds. (p96)

Seljalandsfoss Explore behind falls thundering next to the Ring Road. (p96)

Snæfellsjökull National Park Ice caps, lava fields, native flora and coastal walks, some led by rangers for free. (p110)

Jökulsárlón Jaw-dropping glacial lagoon with icebergs like floating sculptures. (p104)

Best Art & Architecture

Hallgrímskirkja Wander the church grounds and look inside, though the tower will cost ya. (p50)

Viðey Island Art installations such as Yoko Ono's *Imagine Peace Tower* and Richard Serra's *Milestones*. (p70)

Einar Jónsson Sculpture Garden Check out 26 bronzes in the shadow of Hallgrímskirkja. (p57)

Sun Voyager One of many public sculptures in Reykjavík, this one sits along the capital's coastline. (p57)

Harpa Wander the faceted glass interior of the monumental concert hall. (p55)

Best Local

Reykjavík Botanic Gardens Grassy fields and thousands of sub-Arctic plants and flowers. (pictured above; p69)

Whale Watching in Garður Picnic on Reykjanes Peninsula headlands while watching for whales, seals and migrating seabirds. (p75)

Valahnúkur Climb the cliffs and see bubbling geothermal springs at the tip of Reykjanes Peninsula. (p75)

Reykjanesfólkvangur Wilderness Reserve Hike trails by bird cliffs, mineral lakes and multicoloured geothermal fields. (p75)

FEARGUS COONEY / GETTY IMAGES ©

☑ **Top Tip**

▶ At the time of writing many of Iceland's natural wonders were free, but there is talk of introducing fees, ensuring travellers contribute to the protection and maintenance of natural sites.

Survival Guide

Survival Guide

Before You Go

When to Go

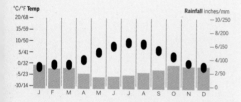

→ **High Season (Jun–Aug)** Visitors descend en masse – especially in Reykjavík and the south. Prices peak and accommodation bookings are essential. Endless daylight, plentiful festivals, busy activities.

→ **Shoulder (May & Sep)** Breezier weather; occasional snows. Optimal conditions for those who prefer smaller crowds, lower prices.

→ **Low Season (Oct–Apr)** Long nights with possible Northern Lights viewings. Winter activities including skiing, snowshoeing, visiting ice caves.

Book Your Stay

→ It's essential to book months ahead for June to August in Reykjavík and the southwest (especially around Vík).

→ Reykjavík 101 is the central district, best for easy walking around town.

→ Reykjavík has a full spectrum of accommodation: from camping and hostels to guesthouses, business hotels, apartments and boutique hotels. All book up in summer; many are open year-round.

→ Prices are high for what you get (and rising fast). Often private apartments are the best bet.

→ Country farmstays offer rooms, beds and/or cottages and are a fun way to overnight out of town.

Useful Websites

AirBnB (www.airbnb.com) Private rooms, apartments and houses; often the best deal in the capital.

Booking.com Very popular and thorough, especially in the countryside.

Icelandic Farm Holidays (www.farmholidays.is) Top farmstays.

CouchSurfing (www.couchsurfing.com) Network of travellers hosting travellers.

Lonely Planet (www.lonelyplanet.com/iceland/hotels) Author reviews and online booking.

Best Budget

Loft Hostel (www.lofthostel.is) Hip, central and with great nightlife, this is one of the town's best hostels.

Reykjavík Downtown Hostel (www.hostel.is) Top dorm digs or private rooms in this HI hostel offer some of the best bargains in the city centre.

KEX Hostel (www.kexhostel.is) A favourite for its off-beat decor and good bar.

Best Midrange

Forsæla Apartment-house (www.apartmenthouse.is) Cosy B&B rooms or apartments and even a small house get top marks for comfort.

Nest Apartments (http://nestapartments.is) Small, comfortable, well-appointed flats with a great location.

Galtafell Guesthouse (www.galtafell.com) Comfortable doubles and apartments fill a restored, beautiful mansion.

Best Top End

Kvosin Downtown Hotel (www.kvosinhotel.is) Some of these sleek apartments in the heart of Old Reykjavík offer super views.

Black Pearl (www.blackpearlreykjavik.com) Near the Old Harbour, these flats offer full concierge service.

Reykjavík Residence (www.rrhotel.is) Rooms and apartments in beautifully renovated mansions near Laugavegur.

Arriving in Reykjavík

Keflavík International Airport

➜ Three easy bus services connect Reykjavík and the airport (50 minutes), and are by far the best bet; kids get discounted fares. Taxis cost approximately kr15,000.

Flybus (☎580 5400; www.re.is; 🛜) Operated by Reykjavík Excursions, Flybus meets all international flights. One-way tickets cost kr2200. Pay kr2800 for hotel pickup/drop off (which shuttles you from/to the Flybus at the BSÍ bus terminal); you must schedule hotel pick-up a day ahead. A separate service runs to the Blue Lagoon (from where you can continue to the city centre or the airport; kr3900). Tickets online, at many hotels, or at the airport booth.

Airport Express (☎540 1313; www.airportexpress.is; 🛜) Operated by Gray Line Tours between

Keflavík International Airport and Lækjartorg Sq in central Reykjavík (kr2100) or Mjódd bus terminal, or via hotel pickup/drop off (kr2700; book ahead).

Airport Direct (📞497 5000; www.reykjaviksight seeing.is/airport-direct; 📶) Minibuses operated by Reykjavík Sightseeing shuttle between hotels and the airport (kr4500, return kr8000).

➡ Strætó (www.bus.is) bus 55 also connects the BSÍ bus terminal and the airport (kr1680, nine daily Monday to Friday in summer).

Reykjavík Domestic Airport

➡ From the Reykjavík Domestic Airport it's a 2km walk into town, there's a taxi rank, or Strætó (www.bus.is) bus 15 stops near the Air Iceland terminal and bus 19 stops near the Eagle Air terminal. Both go to the city centre and the Hlemmur bus stop.

Getting Around

Local Bus

➡ Strætó (www.bus.is) operates regular, easy buses around Reykjavík and its suburbs with main stops at Hlemmur, at the eastern end of Laugave-gur, and Lækjartorg Sq, in the centre of town.

➡ Many buses make a loop around Tjörnin lake and serve the centre, National Museum and BSÍ bus terminal before heading on.

➡ Mjódd, 8km southeast of the city centre, is the main bus terminal, and where you catch long-distance Strætó buses.

➡ Online schedules, smartphone app and a printed map. Many free maps like *Welcome to Reykjavík City Map* also include bus-route maps.

➡ Fare is kr420; buy tick-ets at the bus terminal, on board (though no change is given) or by using its app. Transfer tickets (from the driver) are good for 75 minutes.

➡ One-/three-day passes (kr1500/3500) are sold at Mjódd bus terminal,

tourist offices, many hotels and bigger swim-ming pools.

➡ Buses run 7am until 11pm or midnight daily (from 11am on Sunday) at 20-minute or 30-minute intervals. Limited night-bus service runs until 2am on Friday and Saturday.

Car

➡ Totally unnecessary in central Reykjavík.

➡ Roads are good in the most-visited areas.

➡ Book ahead for best deals; if there's two or more of you it can be cheaper than the bus.

➡ Check out Carpooling in Iceland (www.sam ferda.is) and Bílfar (www. bilfar.is).

➡ Many countryside petrol stations are automated; you need a PIN-equipped ATM or credit card. Arrange one before you leave home. If you don't have a PIN, buy prepaid cards from N1 stations to use at automated pumps.

➡ 4WDs only necessary for highland travel (F roads: where 2WD rental cars are forbidden).

➡ Limited parking in the centre; machines accept

coins and ATM or credit cards with PIN only and operate between 9am and 6pm from Monday to Friday and from 10am to 4pm Saturday.

➡ Illegal to use a mobile phone while driving.

Regional Bus & Tours

➡ Single or multiday tours, many offering hotel pick-up, depart from Reykjavík, or use Strætó and the major bus tour companies listed here for transport.

➡ The *Public Transport in Iceland* free map (www. publictransport.is) shows all routes.

➡ The companies offer bus passes, but some are costly and you're then tied to the one service. Do your research: a car can sometimes be cheaper.

➡ From roughly mid-May to mid-September regular scheduled buses go to most places on the Ring Road (Rte 1), into the popular hiking areas of the southwest, and to larger towns on the Reykjanes and Snæfellsnes Peninsulas, Westfjords and Eastfjords. The rest of the year, services range from daily to nonexistent.

➡ In small towns, buses usually stop at the main petrol station.

➡ **Strætó** (☏540 2700; www.bus.is) Operates Reykjavík long-distance buses from Mjódd bus terminal, 8km southeast of the city centre, which is served by local buses 3, 4, 11, 12, 17, 21, 24 and 28. Strætó also operates city buses and has a smartphone app. For long-distance buses only you can use cash, credit/ debit card with PIN or (wads of) bus tickets.

➡ **Reykjavík Excursions** (Kynnisferðir; ☏580 5400; www.re.is; BSÍ Bus Terminal, Vatnsmýrarvegur 10) and its Flybus uses the BSÍ bus terminal (pronounced *bee-ess-ee*), south of the city centre. There's a ticketing desk, tourist brochures, lockers, luggage storage (www. luggagelockers.is), Budget car hire and a cafeteria with wi-fi. The terminal is served by Reykjavík buses 1, 3, 5, 6, 14 and 15. Reykjavík Excursions offers prebooked hotel pickup to bring you to the terminal. Some Gray Line buses also stop here.

➡ **Sterna** (☏551 1166; www.sterna.is; 🛜) Sales and departures from the

Harpa concert hall. Buses around the Ring Road and to tourist highlights.

➡ **Trex** (☏587 6000; www. trex.is) Departs from the Main Tourist Office, Kringlan's Shell petrol station or Reykjavík Campsite. Buses to Þórsmörk and Landmannalaugar.

Air

➡ Domestic flights and those to Greenland and the Faroe Islands leave from Reykjavík Domestic Airport.

➡ **Air Iceland** (Flugfélag Íslands; ☏570 3030; www. airiceland.is) Operates flights and sightseeing services. Book online.

Essential Information

Discount Cards

➡ **Reykjavík City Card** (www.citycard.is; 24/48/72hr kr3500/4700/5500) offers admission to Reykjavík's municipal swimming/ thermal pools and to most of the main galleries and museums, plus discounts on some tours, shops and entertainment. Also gives free travel on the city's Strætó buses and on the ferry to Viðey.

➡ Buy it at the **Main Tourist Office** (Upplýsingamiðstöð Ferðamanna; Map p28; ☎590 1550; www.visitreykjavik.is; Aðalstræti 2; ☻8am-8pm), some travel agencies, 10-11 supermarkets, HI hostels and some hotels.

➡ Kids enter many museums free; the Children's City Card (24/48/72 hours kr1300/2400/3100) covers other services.

Electricity

230V/50Hz

230V/50Hz

Emergency

➡ For emergency services and search and rescue call ☎112.

Money

☑ **Top Tip** While credit cards are ubiquitous, many transactions (such as petrol purchases) require a PIN. Make sure you have one before you leave home.

➡ Icelandic unit of currency is the króna (plural krónur), written as kr here, often written elsewhere as ISK.

➡ Credit cards are used everywhere; ATMs are throughout the centre.

➡ Tipping is not required, as service and VAT (value added tax) are included.

Public Holidays

New Year's Day 1 January

Easter March or April; Maundy Thursday and Good Friday to Easter Monday (changes annually)

First Day of Summer First Thursday after 18 April

Labour Day 1 May

Ascension Day May or June (changes annually)

Whit Sunday and Whit Monday May or June (changes annually)

National Day 17 June

Commerce Day First Monday in August

Christmas 24 to 26 December

New Year's Eve 31 December

Telephone

☑ **Top Tip** For longer stays, or for the mobile addicted, Icelandic SIM cards are cheap and practical; you'll need an unlocked GSM 900/1800 mobile.

➡ Iceland's country code: ☎354 (note: Iceland has no area codes).

➡ Online phonebook: http://en.ja.is.

➜ Buy prepaid SIM cards at bookshops, grocery stores and petrol stations. Iceland telecom Síminn (www.siminn.is/prepaid) provides greatest network coverage; Vodafone (www.vodafone.is/en/prepaid) is not far behind.

➜ Voice-and-data starter packs including local SIM cards; Síminn's costs kr2000 (and includes kr2000 in call credit).

➜ Public phones are elusive.

Tourist Information

☑ **Top Tip** Sites www.visitreykjavik.is and www.grapevine.is have all you need for a short stay; www.visitreykjanes.is, www.south.is and www.west.is cover the countryside.

➜ **Main Tourist Office** (Upplýsingamiðstöð Ferðamanna; Map p28; ☎590 1550; www.visitreykjavik.is; Aðalstræti 2; ⏰8am-8pm) Friendly staff and mountains of free brochures, plus maps and Strætó city bus tickets for sale. Book accommodation, tours and activities.

Travellers with Disabilities

➜ Iceland can be trickier than many places in

Money-Saving Tips

Tax-Free Shopping Anyone who has a permanent address outside Iceland can claim a tax refund on purchases when they spend over kr6000 (at a single point of sale). Look for stores with a 'tax-free shopping' sign in the window, and ask for a form at the register. Full details at www.globalblue.com.

Alcohol Planning on drinking a lot in Reykjavík? Buy liquor at the airport's duty-free shops in the arrivals hall to beat city prices.

northern Europe for travellers with disabilities.

➜ For details on accessible facilities, contact the the National Association of People with Disabilities, **Þekkingarmiðstöð Sjálfsbjargar** (National Association of People with Disabilities; ☎550 0118; www.thekkingarmidstod.is).

➜ God Adgang (www.godadgang.dk) can find accessible service providers.

➜ For tailor-made accessible trips: All Iceland Tours (www.allicelandtours.is) and Iceland Unlimited (www.icelandunlimited.is). Gray Line Iceland (www.grayline.is) has some accessibility options.

➜ Reykjavík's city buses have a 'kneeling' function

so wheelchairs can be lifted on; elsewhere, buses don't have ramps or lifts.

➜ Download Lonely Planet's free Accessible Travel guide from http://lptravel.to/AccessibleTravel.

Visas

➜ Iceland is one of 26 European Schengen Convention countries.

➜ **EU & Schengen countries** No visa required for three months.

➜ **Australia, Canada, Japan, New Zealand & USA** No visa for tourist visits up to three months. Total stay within Schengen area must not exceed three months in any period of six months.

➜ **Other countries** Check online at www.utl.is.

Language

Most Icelanders speak English, however, any attempts to speak the local language will be much appreciated. If you read our pronunciation guides as if they were English, you'll be understood.

Basics

Hello.
Halló.　　ha·loh

Good morning.
Góðan daginn.　　gohth·ahn dai·in

Goodbye.
Bless.　　bles

Thank you
Takk./ Takk fyrir.　　tak/ tak fi·rir

Excuse me.
Afsakið.　　af·sa·kidh

Sorry.
Fyrirgefðu.　　fi·rir·gev·dhu

Yes.
Já.　　yow

No.
Nei.　　nay

How are you?
Hvað segir þú gott?　　kvadh se·yir thoo got

Fine. And you?
Allt fínt. En þú?　　alt feent en thoo

What's your name?
Hvað heitir þú?　　kvadh hay·tir thoo

My name is ...
Ég heiti ...　　yekh hay·li ...

Do you speak English?
Talar þú ensku?　　ta·lar thoo ens·ku

I don't understand.
Ég skil ekki.　　yekh skil e·ki

Directions

Where's the (hotel)?
Hvar er (hótelið)?　　kvar er (hoh·te·lidh)

Can you show me (on the map)?
Geturðu sýnt mér (á kortinu)?　　ge·tur·dhu seent myer (ow *kor*·ti·nu)

What's your address?
Hvert er heimilisfangið þitt?　　kvert er *hay*·mi·lis·fan·gidh thit

Eating & Drinking

What would you recommend?
Hverju mælir þú með?　　kver·yu mai·lir thoo medh

Do you have vegetarian food?
Hafið þið grænmetisrétti?　　ha·vidh thidh grain·me·tis·rye·ti

I'll have a ...
Ég ætla að fá ...　　yekh *ait*·la adh fow ...

Cheers!
Skál!　　skowl

I'd like a/the ..., please.
Get ég fengið ..., takk.　　get yekh fen·gidh ..., tak

table for	*borð fyrir*	bordh fi·rir
bill	*reikninginn*	rayk·nin·gin
drink list	*vínseðillinn*	veen·se·dhit·lin
menu	*matseðillinn*	mat·se·dhit·lin
that dish	*þennan rétt*	the·nan ryet

Emergencies

Help!
Hjálp! hyowlp

Go away!
Farðu! far·dhu

Call ...!
Hringdu á ...! hring·du ow ...!

a doctor
lækni laik·ni

the police
lögregluna leu·rekh·lu·na

I'm lost.
Ég er villtur/villt. (m/f)
yekh er vil·tur/vilt

Where are the toilets?
Hvar er snyrtingin? kvar er snir·tin·gin

Numbers

1	*einn*	aydn
2	*tveir*	tvayr
3	*þrír*	threer
4	*fjórir*	fyoh·rir
5	*fimm*	fim
6	*sex*	seks
7	*sjö*	syeu
8	*átta*	ow·ta
9	*níu*	nee·u
10	*tíu*	tee·u
20	*tuttugu*	tu·tu·gu
30	*þrjátíu*	throw·tee·u
40	*fjörutíu*	fyeur·tee·u
50	*fimmtíu*	fim·tee·u
60	*sextíu*	seks·tee·u
70	*sjötíu*	syeu·tee·u
80	*áttatíu*	ow·ta·tee·u
90	*níutíu*	nee·tee·u
100	*hundrað*	hun·dradh

Shopping & Services

I'm looking for ...
Ég leita að ... yekh lay·ta adh ...

How much is it?
Hvað kostar þetta? kvadh kos·tar the·ta

That's too expensive.
Þetta er of dýrt. the·ta er of deert

Transport

Is this the ...
Er þetta ... er the·ta ...
to (Akureyri)?
til (Akureyrar)? til (a·ku·ray·rar)

boat
ferjan fer·yan

bus
rútan roo·tan

plane
flugvélin flukh·vye·lin

What time's
Hvenær fer ... kve·nair fer ...
the ... bus?
strætisvagninn? strai·tis·vag·nin

One ... ticket (to Reykjavík), please.
Einn miða ... (til Reykjavíkur), tak.
aitn mi·dha ... (til rayk·ya·vee·kur) takk.

How much is it to ...?
Hvað kostar til ... ? kvadh kos·tar til ...

Please stop here.
Stoppaðu hér, takk.
sto·pa·dhu hyer tak

Please take me to (this address).
Viltu aka mér til (þessa staðar).
vil·tu a·ka myer til (the·sa sta·dhar).

Behind the Scenes

Send Us Your Feedback

We love to hear from travellers – your comments help make our books better. We read every word, and we guarantee that your feedback goes straight to the authors. Visit **lonelyplanet.com/contact** to submit your updates and suggestions.

Note: We may edit, reproduce and incorporate your comments in Lonely Planet products such as guidebooks, websites and digital products, so let us know if you don't want your comments reproduced or your name acknowledged. For a copy of our privacy policy visit lonelyplanet.com/privacy.

Alexis' Thanks

My work on Iceland was a labour of love supported by many. Big thanks to Heimir Hansson (Westfjords), Jón Björnsson (Hornstrandir), Dagný Jóhannsdóttir (Southwest), Kristján Guðmundsson (West), Ragnheiður Sylvía Kjartansdóttir (Reykjavík and everywhere!), Einar Sæmundsen (Þing-vellir) and Helga Garðarsdóttir (Lau-gavegurinn). Svava Guðjónsdóttir kept my statistics accurate. Edda and Páll made Húsafell so, so special! Carolyn was once again a brilliant, generous, astute collaborator. Respect to James for his great care. Rachel, Jenny, Oren and Timothy were amazing BOB-sters, making Icelandic escapades a family adventure. Ryan = peachy.

Acknowledgements

Cover photograph: *Solfar (Sun Voyager)* by Jon Gunnar Arnason, Christian Kober/Getty©
Photograph on pp4–5: Hallgrímskirkja, Jay Yuan/shutterstock

This Book

This 2nd edition of Lonely Planet's *Pocket Reykjavík* guidebook was researched and written by Alexis Averbuck. The previous edition was also written by Alexis. This guidebook was produced by the following:

Destination Editor
James Smart

Product Editors
Vicky Smith, Anne Mason

Senior Cartographer
David Kemp

Book Designer
Wendy Wright

Assisting Editors
Andrea Dobbin, Victoria Harrison

Cover Researcher
Naomi Parker

Thanks to
Sasha Baskett, Arne Bergmann, Joel Cotterell, Susan Paterson, Kirsten Rawlings, Tony Wheeler, Tracy Whitmey, Mark Zaslona

Index

See also separate subindexes for:

⊗ **Eating p156**

➈ **Drinking p157**

✪ **Entertainment p157**

⊕ **Shopping p157**

Sights p000
Map Pages **p000**

Sights p000

Map Pages **p000**

☻ Eating

Our Writers

Alexis Averbuck

Alexis Averbuck has travelled and lived all over the world, from Sri Lanka and India to Mexico, Europe and Antarctica. In more recent years she's been living in Hydra, Greece, and exploring her adopted homeland; travelling to France to sample oysters in Brittany and career through hill-top villages in Provence; and adventuring along Iceland's surreal lava fields, sparkling fjords and glacier tongues. A travel writer for over two decades, Alexis has lived in Antarctica for a year, crossed the Pacific by sailboat and written books on her journeys through Asia, Europe and the Americas. She's also a painter – visit www.alexisaverbuck.com. You can also view her profile at https://auth.lonelyplanet.com/profiles/alexisaverbuck.

Contributing Writer

Carolyn Bain contributed to the South Coast and planning chapters of this guide.

Published by Lonely Planet Global Limited
CRN 554153
2nd edition – May 2017
ISBN 978 1 78657 548 7
© Lonely Planet 2017 Photographs © as indicated 2017
10 9 8 7 6 5 4 3 2 1
Printed in China